Blame Teachers

*The Emotional Reasons
for Educational Reform*

A volume in
Studies in the Philosophy of Education
John E. Petrovic, *Series Editor*

Blame Teachers

*The Emotional Reasons
for Educational Reform*

Steven P. Jones
Missouri State University

INFORMATION AGE PUBLISHING, INC.
Charlotte, NC • www.infoagepub.com

Library of Congress Cataloging-in-Publication Data

A CIP record for this book is available from the Library of Congress
http://www.loc.gov

ISBN: 978-1-68123-218-8 (Paperback)
         978-1-68123-219-5 (Hardcover)
         978-1-68123-220-1 (ebook)

Printed in the United States of America

In memory of my parents,
Roy W. and Ila Marie Jones

and for my wife,
Jackie

Contents

Introduction

There is a story going around about the public schools and the people who teach in them. It isn't a very nice story so people don't always tell it openly, but the message gets conveyed, nonetheless. The story circulates especially among educational reformers, state legislators, national and state education officials, businessmen, business groups, and radio talk-show hosts, but many parents and citizens also tell it. The story blames teachers for the state of our American public schools. The story goes like this:

> Our public schools are awful. Proof of this is all around us. Look at the number of schools that under No Child Left Behind failed to make Adequate Yearly Progress (AYP). One international test after another shows that students in the United States perform below—sometimes far below—students in other advanced countries, especially students from our competitors in the global marketplace. Other tests show that huge numbers of students in urban areas are well below grade level in math and reading, and the achievement gap continues to widen between white (and Asian) students and their black and Hispanic counterparts. Graduation rates for minority students are alarming. More and more entering college students have such deficient math and reading skills that they have to take remedial reading and mathematics courses before they can begin their actual college programs.

> We know why our public schools are so awful. The biggest reason is that the teachers teaching in them are so bad. It's not that there are not excellent teachers in the public schools—certainly there are. But the public schools are full of too many bad or merely adequate teachers. Too many teachers don't work hard enough, aren't skilled enough, or settle for far too little

achievement from students. The best and the brightest of our college graduates are not choosing teaching as a career—instead, teaching attracts the less motivated, the less talented, the less intelligent. And instead of weeding out the bad or barely adequate teachers from their comfortable teaching jobs, we have a system in place that protects them. Tenure laws and teachers' unions make it almost impossible to get rid of bad teachers.

Clearly, this must change. We can no longer accept or afford public schools that are so bad. We must get rid of bad teachers and hire better ones. We must embrace new ideas for the public schools like charter schools and privatizing education—ideas that will challenge teachers to perform better. We must close down failing public schools. We need to get rid of tenure laws and teachers' unions, and we need to evaluate teachers with clear-cut data about student performance. We need to attract better people to teaching and quit relying on college and university teacher education programs that have been miserable failures. And we must do these things now before it is too late.

This isn't just a side-story we tell about our schools and teachers—this is *the* story being told about them. It is, I contend, the dominant public narrative about public education in this country.

It doesn't matter if this story is true or not. The people who want to tell this story can find enough facts to make it sound true to those who hear it. What matters is the emotional resonance of the story—what the story makes us feel about teachers when we hear the story being told. And what it makes us feel, mostly, is a sense of betrayal and resentment aimed at teachers. How dare teachers be so self-interested and self-protective as to allow teaching and learning in classrooms to become so degraded!! And how could we let teachers do this to our children?! The "blame teachers" story makes us resentful. And once blame and resentment are at hand, reformers and their supporters have what they need to effect real and substantive change in schools and teaching. They have e*motional reasons* for the educational reforms they propose.

People see and respond to this blame story in different ways. Teachers, of course, are not about to accept so much of the blame for the state of the public schools, and they are not going to admit they are largely incompetent, uncommitted, unenthused, and ineffective. The disavowal of this story is less clear for others who are closely involved with teachers and schools. Most school administrators, school district officials, school board members and state education officials aren't going to endorse this story openly, even if they believe it, but their positions require them to support and implement reforms coming their way. The most virulent dissent to this story comes from people who view education, and these reforms, from a liberal, leftist perspective. The prism of the liberal critique often sends dissenters off to look for capitalistic motives and social injustice within the reforms, and once they go off looking, they usually find something—for-profit charter schools with stockholders presumably making lots of money, robbed local school budgets, and much more. Even those who support educational reform don't always respond to the blame teachers story in the same way. Adamant and aggressive educational reformers want to celebrate and expand every aspect of this story in every public forum they can find. They promulgate the story because they want to accelerate the rate and scope of educational change. But other, less bellicose and more tactical reformers artfully deny they blame teachers for the state of our schools. People like Arne Duncan, Secretary of Education in the Obama administration, try to put a positive spin on all the changes they want. They claim quality teachers should and will embrace the changes being proposed.

This book argues that blame and resentment sit among the key players in this educational drama, quietly festering and moldering. Teachers feel it, school officials evade it, teacher educators want to overlook it, and reformers proclaim or deny it. It would be easier on us all if blame and resentment were not at hand in our discussion of teachers and schools. Emotions like blame and resentment seem a little too petty, a little too unstable, and a little too unreasonable or unjustifiable to admit to as reasons for making big changes in the public schools. It's easier to overlook these things, or at least to pair them with presumed facts. Certainly we have yet to think through the blame and resentment of teachers, though some progress in this direction is made in the pages that follow.

Understanding Blame

Blame is a heavy word. It carries a lot of weighty consequences, and it carries a moral load, as well. We seem to know instinctively that to blame someone for something is a serious matter. There is often something very dear at stake when blame needs to be, or is, assigned for something that has happened. The guilty little glutton who blames his sister for eating the last chocolate chip cookie knows this, and so, too, does the engineer who may be held responsible for a safety violation that leads to some sort of tragedy. Resentment is an even heavier word, a more profound concept. Blame can become resentment when more than cookies are at stake, and there is certainly more at stake than that when we talk about teachers, student learning and the public schools.

We need to be clear about why so many people blame teachers and why so many people come to resent them. This deserves our careful attention.

1

Justifying Reforms and Changes to the Teaching Profession

If teachers are the problem—which is the argument being made by educational reformers and many others—then there really is only one solution: we must change teaching, and change teachers. We see an expanding frustration with teachers and note a broad set of political, economic, and social ideas that support the particular changes to teaching that reformers want to make. Teaching must change, and reformers know how to make it happen.

But educational reformers, state legislators and fed-up citizens are not especially interested in, nor are they positioned to remake, teaching in any technical sense—they generally don't have the technical expertise to tell teachers *how* they should teach or what they should be doing in the classroom. There are exceptions to this, of course. In her book *The Death and Life of the Great American School System: How Testing and Choice are Undermining Education*, Diane Ravitch documents how artful reformers like Anthony Alvarado married educational ideas from the pedagogical left to ideas from

Blame Teachers, pages 1–13
Copyright © 2015 by Information Age Publishing

1

the political right, instituting reading programs like Balanced Literacy that had a significant effect on teachers' practices.[1] But most reforms are being authored and promoted by people outside of education, and so they rarely involve significant pedagogical innovation. Because these reforms don't touch matters of educational practice, input from teachers or other people who have some right to claim a certain expertise in matters of curriculum and pedagogy is not needed—and not wanted.

Reformers tend to agree that past efforts to change public education have had a fatal flaw: they have been conducted almost exclusively by educators. We have known for a long time what is wrong with the *education system*, these critics say, and we have relied on people within that system to fix it. They have proven themselves unable or unwilling to respond to the challenge. Now, certain political and economic realities, together with a renewed concern about the state of our schools and a renewed faith in American entrepreneurial spirit in connection with education, have given us an opportunity to address long-standing educational failures. Now is the time for change, and that time shall not be forgone.

Because teachers and other educators have not been able to clean up their own house, others have stepped in. This reform effort has leading spokespeople, especially Arne Duncan, United States Secretary of Education in the Obama administration. Michelle Rhee, past Chancellor of the Washington D.C. school district, founder of Students First (a group dedicated to educational reform), and now chair of a charter school chain, has certainly been a central figure. So, too, are Joel Klein, past Chancellor of the New York City Department of Education and now Executive Vice-President of Rupert Murdock's News Corporation, and Wendy Kopp, founder and board chair of Teach for America. Groups like the Chicago Public Education Fund and the Bill and Melinda Gates Foundation lend financial support to particular change ideas. Change gets pushed and furthered by the entrance of charter school entrepreneurs on the educational scene—people such as Mike Feinberg and Dave Levin, co-founders of KIPP (Knowledge is Power Program).

But the push for these changes also has the feel of what, in political terms, we might call a *groundswell*—that is, it seems to emanate not just from key figures, but from closer to home. State legislators and members of state and local school boards are the key people actually making changes, not just proposing them, and they act as they do with some significant approval from their constituents. Calls for educational change are not just issued by people sitting at well-financed and influential policy roundtables. They are issued by people sitting at their kitchen tables, too.

Bad Teachers, Teachers' Unions, and the System

If most people advocating for change in the teaching profession will never openly admit they blame and resent teachers for the state of our public schools, they have other ways to express their frustration with teachers. We have all heard critics declaim about *bad* teachers, teachers' unions, or *the system* as a whole—targets for criticism and change, we might say, that are in and around all teachers without appearing to be aimed directly *at* them. We will encounter a fourth way to couch criticisms of teachers and teaching in a vision of a remade teaching profession when we take a careful look at a speech from Arne Duncan in Chapter 3. But, first, a quick look at the other three ways to shape blame.

It is often the case that when a critical note about teachers is sounded in the writings or remarks of reform advocates, that criticism is professed to be aimed at bad or poor-performing teachers, and certainly not at great or even capable teachers. This qualified or measured criticism of teachers is presented as the kind of criticism anyone who looks at teaching in a fair and unbiased way might offer. There are good teachers and bad teachers, critics say. Good teachers need to be praised and supported, but bad teachers need to be identified and either helped to improve or be removed from the profession. And while removal of tenure and union protection is designed to make it easier to fire bad teachers, other changes to the profession, such as merit pay, are designed to reward good teachers. These changes, reformers claim, aren't being proposed by people who hate teachers—we should *all* want to improve teaching, and, therefore, we should all embrace these changes, teachers included. Our children need excellent teachers and are depending on us to make necessary changes.

Or reform advocates can take another tack in demanding changes to the profession of teaching without blaming teachers: they can blame teachers' unions. In a 2011 speech at the Brookings Institute, Chris Christie, governor of New Jersey, outlined changes to teaching he believes need to be made. Governor Christie made it clear at the opening of his speech that he doesn't hate teachers:

> Let's talk first about what this issue really is and what it isn't. This is not an issue about attacking teachers. This is not an issue about saying teachers are bad and need to be thrown out of schools. This is, in fact, exactly the opposite. This issue is about first and foremost our children and how much those teachers who really are good and really care about education, how they can be empowered to teach those children and prepare them better for higher education or for a career.[2]

Later in his speech, however, Christie minces no words about teachers' unions. Teachers' unions are a "moneyed special interest that bullies and thugs its way through the hallways of my statehouse to get whatever it wants." State senators and representatives are afraid to "rustle things up" and alienate teachers' unions whose monetary support they need for re-election. Mimicking legislators who yield to pressure from teachers' unions, Christie said "We don't want to upset a teacher. We don't want to upset, for goodness sakes, their union." Caring more about upsetting teachers or teachers' unions than fixing things for our children is, for Christie, "an obscenity."

A third way politicians and other educational reformers can avoid the appearance of attacking teachers while still arguing for changes to the profession is by attacking *the system* in which teachers work. Here, the problem is not with teachers, but with an out-of-control morass of bureaucratic procedures that gets in the way of teaching and learning. *The system* might include the protections of teachers gained by teachers' unions through collective bargaining—tenure rights and the elongated snarl of dismissal procedures, for instance—but it would also include bloated school district administrative procedures, state and federal regulations and mandated reporting, excessive standardized testing of students, and other "administrivia" that interferes with teachers' efforts in the classroom. Proponents of charter schools use this argument all the time. Being outside the stultifying bureaucratic confusion of large urban public school districts allows charter schools, proponents claim, to work much more effectively and efficiently and return the focus of school administrators and teachers to the learning of students.

The regular use of such qualifications or limitations to the criticism of teachers by educational reformers bent on remaking teaching leaves us in a bit of a tough spot regarding what these reformers actually think about teachers. Certainly, education reformers need to be allowed to qualify their criticism of teachers—they need room to press for change in teaching without necessarily being seen as "anti-teacher." Anyone who wants to comment on or criticize something about teachers and teaching needs a similar allowance. But if we trust the qualifications that politicians and reformers offer to their arguments—that criticism of teachers is limited just to the relatively few bad teachers, or to the teachers' unions, or to the system—then are we to believe that, in the main or in the whole, reformers, politicians, and others still think highly of teachers? Or, by qualifying their remarks as they do, are such critics simply taking advantage of a convenient buffer or safeguard against accusations that they "hate teachers," while, nonetheless, suggesting a broader criticism of teachers?

Reforming the Profession of Teaching

We noted above that most educational reformers don't have the expertise to tell teachers exactly how they should be teaching in the classroom. But if reformers don't know how to or aren't interested in reforming the *practices* of teachers, they are interested in and know how to reform the *profession* of teaching. Reformers typically have three kinds of change in mind—changes, they insist, that are designed especially to solve the problem of bad teachers, teachers unions, and the bureaucratic system of education. As we will see in later chapters, however, these reforms change much more than that.

The first change: Reforming the profession of teaching means, in part, altering the conditions and courtesies that have historically been offered to teachers, especially conditions and courtesies having to do with job security. It means doing away with such things as tenure and "last hired/first fired" practices, and it means dramatically curtailing or eliminating protections and representation by teachers' unions. Reformers want working conditions remade so poor teachers can be easily identified and fired. Value-added assessment practices based on standardized test scores will determine which teachers are doing a good job and which aren't. Excellent teachers should share in merit pay while lesser teachers should not. Merit pay will help remake the profession, reformers believe, by attracting new people to teaching who have been deterred because of low teacher salaries. Money from cuts to traditional health and pension benefits will allow an increase in the starting salary of targeted teachers—math and science teachers, especially, and teachers working in poverty-stricken areas. There just isn't enough money anymore, legislators say, to pay for the generous benefits teachers are accustomed to receiving.

The second change: The changes just mentioned alter the customary professional landscape of teachers and eliminate a comfort level and security teachers have enjoyed—a comfort level and security that reformers see as counterproductive. Behind the elimination of comfort and security lies an implicit argument about teachers themselves—that comfort and security has left them soft, that they do not have the energy, the drive, or the ambition they should have. Reformers want teachers to be tougher than they have been—tougher and more insistent with students, yes, but mostly tougher on themselves. They want them more dogged, more determined, more persistent, more driven. Reformers want teachers who insist on success and who are willing to measure themselves against agreed upon markers of success—especially standardized tests that measure student learning. They want teachers who are so sure of their abilities that they are willing to tie their economic futures to merit pay. Competitive drive is also fostered by charter schools and voucher systems, and by threats to close the lowest performing public schools. And it is certainly fostered by eliminating tenure and union protection. Reformers want teachers to be the kind of people who thrive in a competitive, aggressive environment.

The third change: Finally, proposed reforms circumscribe the tasks of teachers. Reforms center on a teacher's core responsibility—to see that students have learned what has been identified for them to learn. With all manner of standards and accountability measures, including the Common Core State Standards and associated standardized tests, teachers are held in place by a purposeful top-to-bottom system that can include a complete set of curriculum and instructional materials—textbooks, lesson plans, worksheets, supplementary materials, websites, quizzes, tests, etc. Teacher quality is to be determined, in large part, by how well a teacher's students score on standardized tests, and so is the teacher's merit pay. This will ensure teachers keep to the prescribed material. With so much at stake personally for teachers, they will make sure students know how to score well on the tests and will see that they do so.

Stripped bare, the current round of reform has mostly to do with putting pressure on teachers to perform—pressure on school administrators, school boards, and even teacher education institutions, too—but mostly pressure on teachers. Any kind and manner of change designed to produce a "better brand of teacher" is likely to find a home in this climate of educational reform.

Political, Economic, and Other Social Conditions That Support Educational Reform

We can make sense of these proposed (and enacted) reforms within an educational perspective—that is, we can see how reformers have come up with this set of reforms based on their understanding of teachers, students, and the public schools. But these reform ideas are not divorced from other ideas current in our social world. A vast set of political, economic, and social understandings suggest and support the remaking of teaching and reform of schools suggested by educational reformers. We start with a look at the data-intensification of our world made possible by computer technology, then take a quick look at other supporting social ideas.

The Data-Intensification of Our World

It is impossible to over-estimate how the data-intensification of our world has affected teaching and the public schools and how the reliance on data justifies certain educational reforms. It wasn't so long ago that we didn't have the technology to keep track of things as carefully as we do now—technology that helps the businessman keep track of inventory and customers, or that helps transport companies keep track of moving products, or that helps teachers keep track of students' progress. But now we keep track of just about everything, and "getting lost" is no longer tolerated. If we collect the right data, the businessman's products and the teachers' students will be protected. Data is knowledge and knowledge is power—power to do more, to make more money, to be more efficient, to do things better.

Now we want exhaustive, detailed and nuanced data about our schools—especially data about student learning. Many people, including many educators, believe that data about student learning—especially data from standardized tests given to students on a regular basis—allow us, for the first time, to evaluate teachers properly. Data about student learning unmasks teacher performance, advocates believe, and reveals whether or not a given teacher has been effective. We are also able to compare teachers—to talk about better or worse teachers with evidence. All this sets the stage for arguments in favor of new teacher evaluation protocols, merit pay, and doing away with existing policies designed to protect teachers. And, another benefit: Many educators are excited about how all this accumulated data gives teachers an opportunity to individualize instruction for students. Teachers are now often required to give students "before, during, and after" achievement tests carefully crafted to reveal to the teachers (and students, parents, and administrative supervisors) exactly what parts of a particular subject matter students know and understand, and which parts might still confuse them.

But while many are convinced that data is the surest way to put things right and ensure that our schools are serving our students well, others (including lots of teachers) are skeptical. Many teachers are not at all sure that the regular collection of data gives a full and accurate picture of either student achievement or teacher performance—and many do not want such data to be the sole or primary tool in the evaluation of teachers. But resistive teachers are suspect. These teachers invite the accusation that they are "soft"—that they don't want administrators and others to know just how well (or how badly) they are performing in the classroom, that they just want to hide their poor performance from view and rely on tenure and other policies for "protection." This resistance makes reformers even more convinced of the need for data-based decision-making about teacher performance.

Shared American Values

Educational reformers draw on a set of American values they take to be widely shared as they describe problems with teachers and schools and craft their educational reforms. They are no doubt right to assume most Americans share these values, though it is dangerous to assume that all Americans see these values in exactly the same way.

But we often speak of certain ideas as being quintessentially American, starting with our abiding faith in the individual. We believe in the self-sufficient American—the man or woman who, given a fair opportunity, can and will stand on his or her own two feet and make his or her own way in the world. We tend not to believe equal outcomes are the mark of social justice, but we think equal opportunity is. We believe in the power of dreams, and we admire people who have the talent, will, and determination to make their dreams come true. And we believe in the marketplace of ideas. We believe in the power of innovation. We believe that if someone has a better idea about how to do something, that person should be rewarded for it.

We believe in freedom, and we believe in choice as an expression of that freedom. We choose churches, jobs, places to live, ways to raise our families, where we shop, and what we buy. We choose our lovers and our spouses. We choose our friends and our leaders. We choose the political, economic, and social ideas we want to embrace or discard. And so we believe we should be able to choose what schools we send our children to.

Though not so glorious sounding, Americans also believe in accountability. We want an accounting of "value received" in all our transactions, especially those involving public institutions. Accountability always has an economic side to it—we want to see that we are getting what we paid for. But this economic side has a moral equivalent. Accountability ensures people do what it is they have been entrusted to do. We "hold people accountable" when our expectations are not met.

Other Shared American Values

Reformers draw on other social and economic values that, though still widely held, are more problematic and contentious than those just discussed. American faith in competition is one such value. Most Americans believe in the power of competition. Competition in business and industry, we tend to believe, benefits everyone by making better or higher quality goods and services available for less cost. We worry about corporations like Walmart that tend to wipe out local businesses, but we also have faith that competition weeds out inferior or over-priced products as it weeds out inferior and inefficient producers. Reformers and many others believe that if we brought competition to public institutions like health care and the public schools, we would enjoy the same benefits. We would be better off if these bloated and inefficient governmental bureaucracies were privatized.

Many Americans believe the private sector responds better to the changing dynamics of the marketplace and better judges the productivity of workers than the more protective public sector, especially public schools that involve not only unions, but guaranteed tenure rights. In the private sector, the argument goes, all workers receive protection from labor laws (if not from unions) but employers have greater latitude in rewarding excellent workers and firing workers who perform poorly. Private employers can make adjustments on the fly and so they operate more efficiently and economically. Aggressive education companies with a firm and committed vision believe they can attract better people into teaching by promising them a position that is unencumbered by stagnant retention and promotion policies.

A scarcity of jobs—including teaching jobs—tends to dissipate or mute arguments, especially among the young, against the privatization of the public schools that would bring with it the elimination of unions and tenure. Young people who want to teach want jobs, and they will take them in charter schools that offer little or no job protection when they can't find teaching positions in traditional school districts. The supply and demand of teachers is but one economic factor on which reformers rely. They also capitalize on our growing fears about America's place in the global economy. When international education comparisons show our children falling behind the children of our competitors in the global economy—whether or not the tests are precisely right or fair—we start to take a hard look at schools and the key people in them. Where we find reason to blame teachers, reformers gain support for their proposals.

Finally, education reformers draw upon the economic understanding and political will of a sizeable number of citizens and politicians that has taken shape since the economic downfall of 2008 and the rise of the Tea Party prior to the 2010 elections. The arguments in these last years about the evils of big government—about government interfering in the marketplace by bailing out private companies deemed "too big to fail"; about Obamacare and the nationalization of healthcare; about rising federal deficits and how increasing taxes is not the answer—all contribute to a feeling that "big" public school districts aren't the answer, either. We need to be leaner and meaner—we need to get by with less. We need aggressive private enterprise, not government largesse. And it doesn't help when citizens who hold these views see teachers as insulated from the economic hardship of others in a government job that protects their employment.

Civil Rights and Social Justice

In making the argument for educational reform, reformers also draw on two related social values that are very different from the others mentioned above. They frame their argument in terms of civil rights and social justice. Students attending public schools have a right to expect those schools will prepare them to live happy, secure, and productive lives. But, reformers insist, this isn't happening in many schools. Too many of our children, especially the most vulnerable among them, are having their life chances ruined because of the schools they attend. Students have a right to something better.

Reformers made this civil rights argument in the *Vergara vs. California* court case in June 2014. In the case heard before the California Supreme Court, nine plaintiffs sued the state, arguing that California's laws having to do with tenure, protection of seniority rights, and "last hired/first fired" dismissal laws denied them their right to a quality education. In particular, the plaintiffs argued these laws disproportionately harmed poor and minority students. The judge in the case agreed, ruling these teacher protection statues prevent schools from acting in the best interests of students. The lawsuit was financed largely through an organization called Students Matter, with that organization funded by David Welch, a wealthy businessman. Russlynn Ali, assistant Secretary of Education under Arne Duncan from 2009–2012, testified on behalf of the plaintiffs.

Teachers don't care about the poor and dispossessed—reformers do. That's the argument made in the *Vergara* case, and that's the argument reformers make, or imply, as they press for changes to schools and teaching. Children living in poverty face problems and difficulties that many other children do not, and they deserve teachers who will work hard for them. All children deserve people who protect them and look out for their interests. And if teachers cannot or will not do this, reformers will. This is an argument for civil rights and social justice, and it has the strongest moral appeal of any of the arguments put forth by educational reformers.

Core American Values and the Blame and Resentment of Reformers

These major themes of American social, political, and economic life support educational reform and educational reform talk. These themes put educational reform on powerful footing and give educational reformers all manner of confidence both that these reforms are right and appropriate and that the American people will be receptive to them. These reforms are in accord with common sense shaped by core American values.

Those who would oppose some or all of the proposed educational reforms are left looking like people who oppose these core American values. At least they are left open to such accusations, actually made or clearly implied. How could anyone be against using good solid, reliable data about student achievement in order to determine something important about the quality of a teacher? How could anyone not want to encourage the development of new, innovative and potentially powerful educational ideas by turning loose the power of innovation from the private sector? How could anyone support protective teachers' unions and tenure policies when we all know that there are some really bad teachers who need to be identified and fired? How could anyone not support efforts to make things better for the poor and dispossessed among us? Only people who do not truly believe in the power of the identified values, above, could hold such positions. Or people who are weak and lack ambition or drive—people who prefer the ease and anonymity of governmental employment and the security of union membership.

Manichaean thinking pervades the educational reform conversation: "Either you support these American values and the ideas for educational reform that emanate from them, or you do not." You're either with us, or you're against us. Some educational reformers tend to see their ideas, and resistance to those ideas (especially from teachers), in moralistic and overly simplistic terms of "Good versus Evil." Reformers have found the good and are crusaders for it. Anything, or anyone, which impedes these educational reforms is, by definition, on the side of evil.[3]

Reformers are buttressed in this Manichaean approach because it is ever-present in our political lives. President George W. Bush's response to the 9/11 tragedy is the most famous recent example of this kind of thinking: "Either you are with us or you are with the terrorists," he said to a joint session of Congress on September 20, 2001.[4] Such language is intended to identify and celebrate core values or rally people in times of turbulence or trouble. Now we see this language in debates about the size of government and the management of our economy—in arguments about taxes, spending, and entitlements. The Tea Party came to be a considerable political presence based precisely on either/or thinking. Tea Partiers have no middle ground when it comes to taxes, entitlements, and the size of government; and Tea Party leaders are adept at targeting even their own professed supporters who violate any aspect of the accepted code. You will sign the "no new taxes" pledge, or you will be challenged in the next primary election. You are on the side of American faith in the private sector and the power of the individual; or you are on the side of those who would deny the power and efficacy of those values. You're with us or you're against us. And now we hear the same kind of either/or talk from educational reformers.

This generalization about the Manichaean thinking of educational reformers may be thought unfair. "Good" and "evil" may seem too radical and prejudicial a way to characterize the divide educational reformers find between those on "their side" and those resistant to, or skeptical about, proposed reforms—especially teachers. But the two terms reveal not only the starkness of the educational choices reformers believe we face, but something about the people making those choices. A perceived rejection of core American values or an indifferent disregard of those values is for reformers and others an *occasion for resentment*. (The idea of resentment is explored in some depth in Chapter 2.) We become morally indignant or disapproving when we detect, or we think we detect, a permanent register of attitudes and intentions that denies core American values. If teachers (or others) reject the reforms conceived out of those fundamental values, then they must reject those fundamental values—at least as they pertain to education.

But rejecting or being indifferent to American values like the power of the private sector and the virtues of capitalism is one thing. Rejecting or being indifferent to the ideals of social justice and refusing to assist the underprivileged (or appearing to be so inclined) is quite another. In their public arguments for educational reform, reformers wed the ideal of social justice and concern for the poor to these other prominent American values, arguing that these American values, applied to education, will solve many or all of the social and educational problems of the poor. So when teachers (or anyone else) reject these educational reforms, they look like they are willing to subject the poor and dispossessed not only to a continuing substandard education, but to a continuing life of poverty and distress. Reformers can claim that teachers choose their own self-interest over the interests of those they should be serving. A perceived refusal to help the poor and indigent in favor of preserving one's self-interest is the exact recipe for blame and resentment—and for educational reform. We cannot and will not tolerate this, especially from teachers, and moral condemnation is the result.

If this is not "good" versus "evil," it is something close to it. Or, so it can be portrayed by educational reformers and heard by much of the American public.

Notes

1. Diane Ravitch, *The Death and Life of the Great American School System: How Testing and Choice are Undermining Education* (New York, NY: Basic Books, 2011), 31–46.

2. Chris Christie, "2011: The Year of Education Reform" (keynote address at an event sponsored by the Brookings Institution in Washington D.C., April 7, 2011), accessed October 25, 2014, http://www.brookings.edu/events/2011/04/07-education-christie.

3. Thanks to David Owen, who helped shape my thinking on how Manichean thinking shapes all manner of thinking about schools. See David Owen, "Why Do Kids Hate School? A Question of Context." In *Why Kids Hate School*, ed. Steven P. Jones et al. (Dubuque: Kendall/Hunt Publishing, 2007), 29–30.

4. George H. W. Bush, "Address to a Joint Session of Congress and the American People," accessed January 14, 2015, http://georgewbush-whitehouse.archives.gov/news/releases/2001/09/20010920-8.html

$$2$$

Blame and Resentment

There is enough heat in the debate between teachers (and their defenders) and those who want to remake teaching to remind some commentators of the nastiness of the debate about abortion.[1] This may seem like an exaggeration, but the comparison can be instructive. Heat signals that something important is at stake. Heat signals that those involved aren't just playing, aren't just positioning themselves relative to some fairly insignificant issue. If nothing as serious as the sanctity of human life or our right to choose is being debated here, the sense of righteous indignation coming from both sides in this educational debate clearly signals a felt violation of something deeply held. This *violation of something deeply held* is more like our moral or ethical position that gets insulted in the abortion debate than it is like, for instance, a momentary loss of self-esteem when someone hurls an off-hand insult our way. This is the violation felt when serious blame is at hand. The second part of this chapter looks at this through the perspective of P. F. Strawson's ideas about resentment.

But we start with our own experiences with blame, tying that to how we commonly think about blaming teachers. Each of us knows blame inti-

Blame Teachers, pages 15–30
Copyright © 2015 by Information Age Publishing
All rights of reproduction in any form reserved.

mately. We know about blame because we have experienced it from an early age. And we know blame from both sides—from the side of someone who has been blamed for something, either justly or unjustly, and from the side of someone who has blamed others for something that has happened.

When We Get Blamed for Something

It is never fun to be blamed for something. Sometimes we know we deserve the blame for something, or we are easily convinced that we do, and at other times we believe blame is absolutely and entirely unjustified. When we know we deserve blame, guilt is an almost immediate response. Our guilt can cause us to be very critical of ourselves—we can feel incompetent, or worthless, or, depending on what we have done, like we are some kind of moral failure. We feel embarrassed when we are caught doing something wrong, and we don't want others to judge us at a moment when we have been less than ourselves.

Sometimes we want to deny responsibility for something we have done. We do a quick calculation and consider whether or not we can get away with denying responsibility or blaming someone else. Any hesitation to accept blame we know we deserve damages our best and most noble thoughts of ourselves. We allow ourselves some redemption, even if we have hesitated, when the courageous and ethical side of us moves us to accept responsibility for what we have done. There is no redemption when we try to escape responsibility. When this happens, our initial relief for having "gotten away with it" is usually soon tempered by our anxiety over getting caught in our web of lies, denial and deceit.

There are quite different emotional responses when we are blamed for something we didn't do—or don't believe we have done. Nothing makes us angrier, and we take no greater personal offense, than when we are blamed for something we did not do. Undeserved blame is a personal injustice we cannot tolerate. It cuts us to the bone, tapping a deep and very potent part of us. When our vanity gets assaulted in this way, anger in the form of righteous indignation is the response. We almost immediately resent someone who charges us with something we have not done, and that resentment will not dissipate quickly.

Of course, we also learn at an early age how to feign this righteous indignation. We seem to know instinctively that the surest way to look innocent, even if we really do deserve blame for something, is to act like we are mad and indignant about the charges being leveled against us. This is, of course, the art of the teenager and the petty thief.

When We Blame Someone Else

Anger, in the form of righteous indignation, is even more the emotional response of the one who is justified in assigning blame to someone for something done or not done; that is, it is justified in the blamer, rather than the one blamed. We often respond with anger or righteous indignation when certain expectations we have for another person or persons are not met, or when we are betrayed or deceived by someone. We react with anger because relationships between people depend on trust—on both parties meeting the explicit or tacit agreements between them—and we feel particularly put-upon or abused when that trust is violated. The young wife, for instance, whose husband has threatened their marriage because he has strayed or failed to treat her properly cannot assign blame to him without that anger that is righteous indignation. She had trusted him, had invested faith in him, had counted on him, and he let her down. She has experienced a profound injustice and has been deeply wounded. Her blame will reflect all of her deep emotions. In the same way, an employer may react with anger and indignation when he discovers an employee has stolen something or taken advantage of him in a certain way. We are never surprised to see anger and indignation when blame is being assigned for something that has gone badly wrong.

Playing "The Blame Game"

Neither are we surprised to see people who are pretty deft in handling blame—both in assigning it and receiving it. We often speak of *playing the blame game*, and our experience tells us that some people play the game pretty well.

What bothers us about conceiving blame in terms of a game is what it implies about the motives of the players—that blame isn't assigned for something that has gone wrong based on some even tempered, unbiased assessment of individual or corporate responsibility (if such an objective assessment is possible)—but that it may be assigned for much lesser and ignoble reasons. We know of or can imagine instances where someone gets blamed for something in order to divert attention away from someone else who may actually be responsible for what has happened. Blame can be assigned to someone or some group of people in order to justify a change in relationship. A husband can blame his wife for any manner of offenses because he wants to get a divorce, for example, or corporate bosses can blame employees for lack of productivity because they want to shed salaries and benefits so they can plump the bottom line for stockholders. Blame can be shifted for all manner of self-interest—to avoid legal prosecution, financial responsibility, public embarrassment, or inconvenience—or it can be shifted out of sheer personal vindictiveness. Blaming someone for something is a perfect way to "get him" or her for some perceived offense previously committed.

Our experience with blame also tells us that some people are particularly skilled at shielding themselves from blame or fending it off when it comes their way. Blame is most powerful and effective when it is accepted—when someone admits responsibility for what has happened. But just as some people know instinctively how to deflect criticism away from themselves, so, too, do people know how to deflect blame. "It isn't my fault" is a response that blunts the effect of blame whether or not the person uttering the phrase truly believes he or she is blameless. Sometimes blame just sits in a public place— issued by the blamer, but never picked up by the one blamed.

All this clouds the essential moral end involved with blaming, that part of moral life we call moral responsibility. In real life, in the smallest personal examples and the biggest corporate or societal examples, things go wrong. People make mistakes, accidents happen, and tragedies take place. In the clearest examples, blame is a naming of those responsible for what has happened, and acceptance of blame is the acceptance of responsibility for what has happened. But when blame becomes a game, or is suspected of being a game, everything gets muddled. Then, blame isn't always to be trusted, and neither is denial of blame. What are the real reasons blame gets assigned in one direction and not another? What does the one assigning blame really want to accomplish? Blame starts looking like a tool of the powerful used to achieve their own ends. Or, from the other side, the avoidance or denial of blame looks like the purest example of self-interest, like a blatant act of self-preservation. "Not my fault" is a phrase uttered to defend one's actions, and, above all, to avoid consequences that come with blame—a loss of one's reputation, stature, work or living conditions, money, or possessions. In all of this, moral responsibility goes out the window.

Choosing Not to Assign Blame

Moral responsibility is less *out the window* than *off the table*, so to speak, when we decide quite intentionally *not* to assign blame for something that has happened, however bad or unfortunate that thing may be. This is the tactic used both in some corporate cultures and in therapeutic or counseling settings.[2] In the business environment, the emphasis shifts from holding someone responsible for what has happened to more of a problem-solving approach. The spotlight is not on who did what wrong, but on how the problem can be fixed so it can be avoided in the future. Blame is minimized or softened as much as possible in hopes of maintaining or developing harmonious and productive work relationships. Something very similar happens in therapeutic or counseling sessions involving, for instance, husbands and wives or family units. Existing problems need to be identified so they can be addressed, but the intention is not to blame someone for problems that exist so much as it is to fix the problems so relationships can heal and become satisfying and productive. The faith here is that people are more likely to accept responsibility for what they have done, and work to correct it, when they do not feel like the intention is to assault or penalize them.

Possible Objections to Our Exploration of Blame

So far, so good, we might say in our exploration of blame. We know blame; we've all experienced it and can recognize it when it happens. Sometimes blame is clearly and unambiguously assigned and accepted, and sometimes people choose to play an awful and destructive blame game. And we recognize that blame can bring heat with it—from those doing the blaming and from those being blamed—especially when we believe ourselves to have been deeply wronged or violated.

And we can see the connection between how blame works in our personal lives to how it works, in general, with teachers in the public schools. Teachers under attack or withering criticism can accept responsibility for the identified problems, consider how they might try to wiggle out of trouble, or believe themselves to be unjustly blamed. Signs of righteous indignation on the side of those criticizing teachers suggests those critics believe teachers have betrayed the expectations and the trust teachers have been accorded, and that they need to be held responsible for this failure. And we can suspect that, to some extent, teachers and their critics might be involved in some kind of blame game. Perhaps critics blame teachers for the state of the public schools in order to win favor for school choice, vouchers, diminished benefits for teachers, and the like. Teachers might deny responsibility for the state of our schools out of their own self-interests—because admitting failure will lead to the diminishment of teacher protection from teachers' unions and tenure laws, and because teachers might be asked to work longer, harder, and perform better, and perhaps for less pay than they are getting now. Given that we don't believe we can trust the motives of the players in this game, how will we know where blame properly lies or if it is deserved at all? Or, taking the point from the previous section, can we identify and solve existing problems with teachers and the schools without assigning blame for things—and thus avoid alienating people from one another?

But some readers may suspect we have needlessly complicated our understanding of blame as it relates to teachers. Perhaps we have made too much of it, especially by suggesting that there is a moral aspect to the blame that gets assigned to teachers for the state of our schools. Maybe the *violation of something deeply held* mentioned at the outset of this chapter is really nothing more than hurt feelings, either on the part of teachers or those blaming them. Maybe holding teachers responsible for accomplishing the tasks they have been assigned has nothing to do with morals or moral sentiments. Either you do the tasks you are supposed to do successfully (and behave appropriately) or you don't, and if you don't, some consequences—and some blame—will naturally follow. It isn't personal—it isn't moral. Blame is just a naming of how things really are. And if a certain heat is generated in the process, that's only a sign that all participants have a lot at stake in the issue.

Something like this point of view about blaming teachers is regularly adopted and articulated by those calling for educational reform and the reform of the teaching profession. It is, we might say, a *common sense approach* to viewing the problems of public education. But this understanding leaves out what we noted above, as we were reminding ourselves of our experiences with blame: that sense of righteous indignation that signals we believe ourselves to have been betrayed or wronged by someone. The cut and dried approach to thinking about teachers and teaching, sketched just above, seems to deny these feelings exist or that they have anything at all to do with decisions being made about teachers. This approach assumes it is possible to adopt a cold, calculating approach to discovering failure, assigning blame, and creating solutions—an approach based on a calm assessment of the facts and available options, an approach uncolored and unaffected by feelings of anger or resentment brought about by feelings of betrayal or deception. It assumes a detached, analytical, and judicial approach to the assigning of blame and solving of problems. Here, either reformers simply deny they harbor feelings of resentment or anger aimed at teachers, or they believe themselves able to rise above such feelings and judge things impartially. They believe they are able to set aside or fence off their emotional responses.

Some other possibilities exist, of course. It might very well be that reformers recognize they have these feelings of anger and resentment but don't want to admit them publically. It's easier to effect change when people believe those proposing the changes are not motivated by petty personal feelings or irrational emotions even though those emotions might precisely be what is fueling the passion of the reformer. It is also, of course, possible for reformers to embrace, share, and use their own feelings of anger and resentment. Reformers can admit those feelings in hopes they will be widely shared and so expand the scope and speed of change.

I think this is a pivotal place in our investigation of *blaming teachers*. Is blame this cool, reserved assessment—and so, probably not deserving of the word *blame* at all? Is what I have called blame nothing more than motiveless, resentment-free, and emotionally neutral assessment of resources and possibilities? Or, is there an emotionally or morally laden sense of blame— something to do with something *deeply held*—that is at the heart of these calls for change? In order to assess this properly, we need to take a detour (and I'll keep the detour as short as possible) into the work of P. F. Strawson, an English philosopher who did some groundbreaking work in moral philosophy.

The Goodwill We Expect Others to Show Us

Strawson's 1962 essay "Freedom and Resentment" provides a way of thinking about the issues with which we are struggling.[3] But Strawson's essay isn't at all about teaching. It is a response to philosophers who were engaged in thinking about moral responsibility, especially those who were "over-intellectualizing" the conditions which must be met in order to hold someone morally responsible for his or her actions. This had been a central concern of philosophers (really, *the* essential concern) since conversation started about these things back in the days of Homer, about eighth century BCE. Is man free to choose what he does—free, so he can be held morally responsible for the actions he takes—or, are those actions really out of his control, having been ordained by the gods, or by Fate, or through some sort of scientific determinism? If a man can't freely choose how he acts, you can't hold him morally responsible for his actions.

According to Strawson, the philosophers' near-exclusive concern about the conditions necessary to hold someone morally responsible for his or her actions meant they had lost sight of a crucial human element— the kinds of attitudes and intentions human beings expect from one another when they are engaged in some sort of relationship. All of us are in all kinds of relationships with all kinds of different people. We are in relationships as members of the same family, as colleagues, as friends, as lovers, as people who share a common interest, or "as chance parties to an enormous range of transactions and encounters."[4] In each and every one of these relationships we are especially watchful of the attitudes and intentions of those with whom we are in relationship. That is, we watch them for the attitudes and intentions they exhibit *towards us*. We do this, Strawson writes, perhaps out of our own vanity or self-love, or perhaps out of our need for love or respect—but no matter the reason, these attitudes and intentions are critical to us:

> These simplifications [vanity, self-love, the need for love or respect] are of use to me only if they help to emphasize how much we actually mind, how much it matters to us, whether the actions of other people—and particularly of some other people—reflect attitudes towards us of goodwill, affection, or esteem on the one hand, or contempt, indifference, or malevolence on the other. If someone treads on my hand accidentally, while trying to help me, the pain may be no less acute than if he treads on it in contemptuous disregard of my existence or with a malevolent wish to injure me. But I shall generally feel in the second case a kind and degree of resentment that I shall not feel in the first. If someone's actions help me to some benefit I desire, then I am benefited in any case; but if he intended them so to benefit me because of his general goodwill towards me, I shall reasonably feel a gratitude which I should not feel at all if the benefit was an incidental consequence, unintended or even regretted by him, of some plan of action with a different aim.[5]

Goodwill, affection, or esteem on the one hand, which results in our feeling affection for the person with whom we are having a relationship; or contempt, indifference, or malevolence on the other, which results in our feeling resentful: we're constantly searching out these attitudes and intentions in those with whom we are having a relationship.

Certainly, however, there are *occasions for resentment*—when the goodwill and affection we are expecting from someone doesn't happen, and we receive, or think we receive, something like contempt or indifference.[6] "Why have I been treated so contemptuously or dismissively?," we ask ourselves, as our feelings of resentment well-up immediately. "Why has this person treated me so badly?" When this happens, we typically look for some special considerations that might modify or mollify this feeling or remove it altogether. These are not hard to find. We often find ourselves saying things like "She didn't mean to," or "He didn't know," or "It couldn't be helped." Or, we might think of other instances where we were quick to excuse someone by saying something like "He wasn't himself," or "She's been under a lot of stress lately."[7] We certainly might not have liked what happened to us, but we're not about to sever our relationship with the person who has offended us based on this unfortunate event or display of attitude.

But there are other occasions for resentment that we cannot or do not want to explain away so easily—occasions that would cause a temporary or long-standing change in our relationship with the one (or ones) we perceive have extended to us some sort of ill-will or contemptuous disregard. Here we do not dismiss attitude, intention, or behavior with phrases like "it couldn't be helped," and we do not explain away the violation because the person "had a rough day." When we see ourselves as victims of someone's contempt, indifference, or malevolence that stems not from a temporary condition we want to excuse but from a more permanent register of attitudes or intentions, we change our relationship with that person (or those people).

Strawson suggests we adopt an *objective attitude* toward such people who have offended us, as opposed to our normal *participant reactive attitudes*. Reactive attitudes are "essentially reactions to the quality of others' wills towards us, as manifested in their behavior: to their good or ill will or indifference or lack of concern."[8] *Personal* reactive attitudes come into play when we react to someone's good or ill will *aimed directly at us*. Personal reactive attitudes have a kind of generalized analogue when we react to the qualities of others' wills not towards ourselves, but towards "all those on whose behalf moral indignation may be felt, i.e., as we now think, towards all men."[9] Where we respond to an actual or perceived display of ill will or indifferent regard in our close, personal relationships with resentment, we respond, Strawson claims, with its analogue when we detect the same kind of ill-will aimed at others. We say we are "indignant or disapproving, or morally indignant or disapproving."[10] And just as we do not want to sever our normal personal relationships when some personal occasion for resentment occurs, neither are we inclined to do so when we detect offenses aimed at others—except if those offenses force us to. Then we at least temporarily adopt a very different kind of attitude, the *objective attitude.*[11]

When we detect that more permanent or persistent register of attitudes or intentions, especially in the event of some more serious act of ill-will, we adopt an objective attitude to the offender or offenders. To adopt the objective attitude to another human being is, for Strawson,

> ...to see him, perhaps, as an object of social policy; as a subject for what, in a wide range of sense, might be called treatment; as something certainly to be taken account, perhaps precautionary, account of; to be managed or handled or cured or trained; perhaps simply to be avoided....[12]

We turn to this objective attitude not just in regard to obvious and extraordinary cases—those people suffering from some sort of neurosis or psychosis, or even children who need to be "managed" or "handled":

> But we can sometimes look with something like the same eye on the behavior of the normal and the mature. We have this resource and can sometimes use it; as a refuge, say, from the strains of involvement; or as an aid to policy; or simply out of intellectual curiosity.[13]

We often find our objective attitude and our normal participant reactive attitudes are in tension with one another, given a particular situation that seems to call for these objective attitudes. It's as if we don't want to abandon our normal reactive attitudes in favor of this other very distancing, detached attitude—as if our humanity and our intelligence are at war with one another.[14] And we often vacillate between these attitudes and find it impossible to adopt an objective attitude wholly and permanently, even when faced with an awful situation.

We understand how this works if we think about parents who have to discipline their child for some serious offense that child has committed. Parents may very well feel resentment for something the child has done—they feel as if the child has aimed some contempt or disregard directly at them—and they will take an objective attitude in dealing with the child. A "policy" is exactly what is needed when some serious offense, stemming from a contemptuous attitude, has occurred, and so, too, is a need to "manage," "handle," or "cure" the child. And every parent knows the need in such instances for a "refuge from the strains of involvement." These are all indicators of an objective attitude the parent is now holding in regard to the misbehaving child, but this attitude will not now become the exclusive attitude the parent holds. We want a return to the good, close relationship we have had with the child.

Just as the parent responds to his or her child, so do we all respond to human beings we see as having a register of attitudes and intentions not considerate of our interests or goodwill—either ours, directly, or for others, more generally. Our tip-off or indicator is the resentment or moral indignation we feel at this slight of our interests, and we respond by suspending our normal participant reactive attitudes in favor of an objective attitude. We are not without some tension in doing this—our heart is in some tension with our head—and we do not hold these attitudes in "a pure or unqualified form."[15] Our treatment of these people is a kind of compromise, constantly shifting direction between objectivity and our normal reactive attitudes.[16] It is usually our hope, furthermore, that these objective attitudes—this management or treatment, or these policies—will work to regulate or fix more favorable attitudes and behaviors.[17] We cannot abide the contempt, disdain, or malevolence others show toward us or toward others in our care, and we hope to restore the goodwill and affection they need to show us so our normal relationships can resume.

Finally, according to Strawson, we withdraw *our* goodwill toward an of-fending party or parties, at least temporarily—and so impose policies or treatments or management strategies—in proportion to the moral indigna-tion, disapprobation, or resentment we feel.[18] The level or magnitude of this indignation, disapprobation, or resentment is proportional to what we believe is the magnitude of the injury we have suffered *and* the magnitude of the ill-will, contempt or disregard we judge the offending party or parties have shown us or those in our care. That is, the more we believe ourselves injured by someone—and the more we think someone has shown us ill-will—the more ill-will we show them, and the more we "manage" them. This last idea connects to the first quote from Strawson, above: two differ-ent people could step on my hand and so injure me, but I will resent only the one I thought was deliberately trying to hurt me, not the one who was trying to help me. Attitude and intention are everything.

Now, back to the main road in trying to understand blame and its con-nection to teachers. We have in Strawson's ideas a way to understand how people, especially educational reformers, are viewing teachers—and why they want such a complete overhaul of the teaching profession.

Teachers and Goodwill

Here's the heart of the matter. Many of us believe teachers have nothing like the goodwill, affection, or esteem for us, or for students, that they should have. Rather than these positive attitudes and intentions—attitudes and in-tentions we expect and require in every other relationship we have with people—we believe we regularly see teachers aim toward us, and toward students, at best an indifferent disregard and, often, outright contempt and malevolence. Teachers show their disregard for students when they don't plan or execute lessons well enough, ignore parent concerns, and let too many things slide; contempt never shows more clearly than when teachers defend the protective provisions of their union contracts and refuse to work longer school days or school years. These and other acts of teachers con-vince us that teachers care for themselves far more than they care for us or for students. When we see this disregard, disdain, and contempt aimed at us, we are immediately resentful; when we see these things aimed at others, especially students, we are morally indignant.

We cannot abide these attitudes in teachers. We do not tolerate them in any of our other relationships, and we are not about to accept them in so important and intimate a relationship as exists between teacher and student (or teacher and parent, or teacher and citizen). As much as we would like to excuse teachers for these attitudes and intentions—and as much as we often *do* excuse particular teachers by saying things like "He must have had a bad day," or "She didn't mean to"—we now see these attitudes and intentions as more permanent and persistent attributes of teachers. Seeing no reason to believe these attitudes and intentions will change, and perceiving the harm these attitudes and intentions are doing to us and to others, we do what we do in all our other relationships when faced with this persistent register of attitudes—we step out of the normal relationship we are having. We cease our normal relationship with teachers. We withdraw the goodwill we had extended to them. We feel resentful and morally indignant. We begin to treat teachers the same way we believe they treat us—and our goodwill toward them turns to ill-will, our affection to contempt, and our esteem to disregard. And the more we feel we, and students, have been injured by teachers, and the more we believe the magnitude of injury is related to the magnitude of ill-will teachers have for us, the more ill-will we aim at teachers.

We adopt an objective attitude toward teachers. This isn't easy for us—our humanity and intelligence are at war with one another. We tend to shift back and forth between an objective attitude and our desire to resume normal relationships with teachers, but until and unless teachers come back to us, as it were, and begin to show us the goodwill, affection, and esteem we require, teachers will need to be managed or handled differently than they have been. The strains of involvement with teachers have become unbearable—there just hasn't been the response or the results we require—and so we adopt new policies and new treatment of them. Now we manage teachers differently. We change the profession of teaching. We take things away from them—tenure, union representation, automatic raises in pay—and we find concrete ways to measure their competence or incompetence. We tend not to call these changes *punishments*, but they certainly are measures taken to force teachers to have the regard for us and for students we believe they have neglected. If these changes to teaching and teachers are what it takes to reinstate that proper regard, then that's just what we'll do.

And now we take a breath and see if this sounds right to us.

The Story We Tell about Teachers

This isn't a very nice story. It's even worse than the one I told in the Introduction about why people blame teachers for the state of the public schools. Most of us would rather tell a different story about teachers. We would rather talk about how beloved and respected teachers are, and we would rather tell stories about how hard they work and the good they do.

And if we have to talk about changing teachers and the teaching profession, we would rather not embed those arguments for change in the kind of moral betrayal I have discussed.

But there are reformers, as I mentioned above, who don't mind telling everyone who will listen how teachers have betrayed the public trust. Jay P. Greene, author of *Why America Needs School Choice*, is one such reform advocate. Greene's disdain for teachers is clear in the following description of the "education establishment":

> Why then does Diane Ravitch and the rest of the education establishment assert that markets don't work in K–12 education? Is K–12 education so unusual that it has to be arranged differently from almost every other private, public, and even educational system? No. The reality is that the K–12 establishment's hostility to markets is fueled by raw self-interest disguised as benevolent paternalism. There are more than 6.3 million people currently employed by public schools, of whom 3.2 million are teachers. And the teachers unions boast 4.7 million members (3.2 million for the National Education Association and 1.5 million for the American Federation of Teachers). The power of these unions as well as the jobs, compensation, and worldview of their members are intertwined with the current nonmarket method of delivering education. Given that there are fewer than 113 million full-time workers in the U.S., these 6.3 million public school employees constitute what Abraham Lincoln might have called a "peculiar and powerful interest," significantly distorting the design of our education system.
>
> Of course, the education establishment does not admit to themselves or to others that they are putting the interests of adults ahead of the education of children. On the contrary, they have developed an elaborate set of rationalizations for their opposition to expanded markets in K–12 education, which most of them believe with complete sincerity. Their self-interest encourages self-delusion.[19]

Phrases like "raw self-interest disguised as benevolent paternalism" and "putting the interests of adults ahead of the education of children" are damning enough to teachers, as a whole, as well as to other members of "the education establishment." But this is nothing compared to Greene's not very subtle allusion to Abraham Lincoln's Second Inaugural Address. The "peculiar and powerful interest" Lincoln mentions in that address are the slaveholders in the South—those whose self-interests were so powerful, whose moral and ethical standards were so corrupt, that they would go to war to save their right to enslave other human beings. All 6.3 million public school employees—every teacher, administrator, administrative assistant, custodian, and school bus driver—are, in powerful ways, just like those slaveholders, according to Greene. But at least he is clear and honest about the magnitude of the problem he sees. He sees not just bad teachers, union protection, or bureaucratic mess. According to Greene, all teachers, and everyone else in the education establishment, deserve his, and our, resentment and moral indignation, and they deserve every bit of our objective attitude and the changed policies and practices that come with it.

But the story I have told is too much to admit for most reformers. It makes the discussion about teachers and change uncomfortable. Recall, from above, that most reformers want to claim a detached, analytical, and judicial approach to the assigning of blame and solving of problems. They would say they are proposing changes to teaching not because teachers, in general, have shown some sort of ill-will or contempt, and they would admit no kind of resentment or moral indignation aimed at teachers. They would deny they have withdrawn the goodwill teachers have enjoyed. They want to argue, instead, that the changes being proposed have their home not in the realm of moral sentiments, but in pragmatism: when something is broken, you fix it. It's just that simple.

But Strawson's work, applied to our feelings toward teachers, corrects this understanding, just as his work corrected the thinking of philosophers who wanted to conceive moral responsibility solely in terms of whether or not certain conditions of free choice had been met. In assigning responsibility, or blame, for something that has happened, we cannot leave out the crucial human element—the kinds of attitudes and intentions human beings expect from one another when they are engaged in some sort of relationship. These attitudes and intentions are essential to us. Every human being expects goodwill, affection, and esteem from *everyone* with whom they have a relationship. We constantly assess this goodwill, and we all react the same way when we don't receive it—or don't think we receive it.

Are we to assume that educational reformers, and others supporting educational reform, are somehow immune to this? Or, does it make more sense to assume that they *are*, in fact, constantly assessing this goodwill and that they *do*, in fact, withdraw their own goodwill toward teachers when they feel themselves, and those in their care, slighted? Again, I think there is every good reason for those actively proposing changes to teachers and teaching to deny that they subscribe to anything like this story of why, and for what, we blame teachers. But that doesn't mean we need to believe them. And it doesn't mean that we should trust that the policies and new management of teachers being proposed by educational reformers comes from nothing more than calm, cool, pragmatic thinking. Furthermore, P. F. Strawson's analysis confirms our experience. What we spoke of at the outset of the chapter as a *violation of something deeply held* we can now see as our expectation that people will show us goodwill—that we will see in the attitudes and intentions of people that they care for us, have affection for us, and esteem us. Whether out of our own self-love or our need for love or respect, this expectation *is* deeply held—it is a profoundly human expectation—and a violation of it will always draw resentment or moral indignation from us.

We need to remember, too, that righteous indignation can come from both sides of the relationship—not just from the blamer who feels hurt, but from the one who feels like he is being blamed for something he did not do. The person being blamed for something expects the same kind of goodwill coming his or her way as the one doing the blaming. When we are falsely blamed for something, we believe that goodwill has been withheld, and we meet that violation with the same kind of resentment or moral indignation as in the other case.

Neither does our analysis of blame in these moral terms preclude us from believing that some sort of *blame game* is being played between teachers and educational reformers. In fact, we might assume the resentment the players feel for one another might justify, in their minds, any and all blame games. Dirty tactics are more justifiable when you don't esteem your opponent.

Our Resentment of Teachers

The story I told in the opening paragraphs of the Introduction about why we blame teachers for the state of our schools has now been amended. Yes, we certainly blame teachers for low test scores and because our results in international comparisons seemingly aren't very good—and we blame teachers for lots of other undesirable or unfortunate circumstances having to do with teaching, learning, and the schools. But mostly we blame teachers because we don't think they care anymore. Or, they don't care enough. We resent everything about the circumstances of the teaching profession that indicates that teachers care more about themselves, as Greene argues, than they do about their students. We resent tenure and teachers' unions. We resent the pay scale that has nothing to do with teaching performance. We resent it when teachers object to standardized testing tied to merit pay or when they complain about new measures of teacher effectiveness. And we resent it when teachers bellyache about pay and other benefits. All these things, together with the poor results we see all around us, we take as signals that teachers are not showing us the goodwill we deserve.

And we can't hide the resentment we feel—no matter how hard we try. We see this resentment even in the words of those reformers who deny they harbor such feelings toward teachers, as we'll see in the next chapter.

Notes

1. Richard Whitmire, "Education is the New Abortion: The Battle over School Reform has Turned Dangerously Vitriolic," *NYDailyNews.com*, June 30, 2011, accessed October 25, 2014, http://www.nydailynews.com/opinion/education-new-abortion-battle-school-reform-turned-dangerously-vitriolic-article-1.132343.
2. Don Gray and Jerry Weinberg, "The Blame Game," AYE Conference, posted June 10, 2009, accessed October 25, 2014, http://www.ayeconference.com/the-blame-game/.
3. P. F. Strawson, Freedom and resentment. *Proceedings of the British Academy, 48* (1962): 1–25. Quoted passages taken from http://people.brandeis.edu/~teuber/P._F._Strawson_Freedom_&_Resentment.pdf, accessed October 25, 2014.
4. Ibid., 3.
5. Ibid., 3.
6. Ibid., 4.
7. Ibid., 4.
8. Ibid., 8.
9. Ibid., 9.
10. Ibid., 8.
11. Ibid., 5.
12. Ibid., 5.
13. Ibid., 6.
14. Ibid., 6.
15. Ibid., 11.
16. Ibid., 11.
17. Ibid., 13.
18. Ibid., 12–13.
19. Jay P. Greene, *Why America Needs School Choice* (New York, NY: Encounter Books, 2011), 3–5.

3

Blame, by Any Other Name

Most reform advocates and legislators do not upbraid teachers in public, accusing them of malfeasance, attacking their character, or insulting their knowledge or skills. The more customary line of criticism, as we saw in Chapter 1, takes aim at "bad" teachers, teacher unions, or "the system." But there is a fourth way to couch criticisms of teachers that we will see in the remarks of Secretary of Education Arne Duncan. Direct criticism, and the criticism implicit in change proposals, seems less threatening—or at least less unkind—when it is softened, or veiled, or sweetened in some way. Reformers sometimes take advantage of this, couching reform as a means to "improve the profession" by increasing the pay and prestige of teachers. Such contexts for change may, at some level, indicate that reformers have a genuine desire to work with teachers to improve teaching. At the very least, teachers are more apt to be flattered instead of insulted by this approach. No teacher would want to listen to or work with someone who openly insults him or her, and reformers know that.

I suggested in the first chapter that what reformers want to do, mostly, is remake the "profession" of teaching. We hear that explicitly in the words

Blame Teachers, pages 31–41
Copyright © 2015 by Information Age Publishing

of Secretary Duncan in a speech to the National Board of Professional Teaching Standards entitled "Working toward 'Wow': A vision for a new teaching profession."[1] In this speech, delivered summer, 2011, Duncan calls for real and substantive changes to teaching—the same kind of changes being called for by other reformers.

What isn't nearly so clear in this speech is Duncan's view of teachers. We uncover his opinion of teachers only when we think behind and within the words of his remarks. Duncan's challenge in this speech is to name things that are wrong and people who are underperforming—clearly teachers—without being unjustly critical of them. Or, to put it another way, his task is to be critical of teachers without appearing to criticize them—or at least without demeaning them—this so his continued admiration and respect of teachers can be publicly proclaimed.

Sneaky

But what we discover in a careful look at Duncan's remarks is the elephant in the room—the thing no one wants to admit, especially educational reformers. But it's the thing that everyone else suspects is true. What we see is that even Arne Duncan, U.S. Secretary of Education, doesn't think much of today's teachers. Which leads us to suspect that other reformers, state and federal legislators, and many, many other people—all arguing for the same basic changes to teaching—don't think much of teachers either.

Working Toward "Wow"

Secretary Duncan opens his speech to these NBPTS teachers by sharing a story about a recent newspaper cartoon that had recently been brought to his attention:

> I don't look at newspaper cartoons much, but someone showed me one the other day that got me thinking. It showed a sports fantasy camp with a bunch of athletes standing around waiting to get an autograph from a short, balding guy. One player points to him and says, "I wish I had that kind of money and respect..." Another athlete points to the man and says, "Wow! (pause) A teacher!"
>
> Now this was just a Sunday cartoon—and I know that you're not all short and balding—but the message behind the humor says a lot about America today: We worship our athletes, our entertainers, our movie stars—but it is great teachers who really should trigger a "wow."[2]

Throughout his speech, Secretary Duncan repeatedly compliments the board certified teachers in attendance: "The educators in this room have changed thousands of lives for the better and I couldn't be prouder to address you," Duncan says.[3] Then he outlines the intent of his remarks as follows:

> Teaching must be one of our nation's most honorable professions. Teachers help mold the future every day, having an impact that far outlasts any lesson plan or career. When I meet young people who want to make a difference, change a life, and leave behind a living, breathing legacy, I urge them to teach. Too often, though, bright, committed young Americans—the very people our students need in the classroom—do not answer the call to teach. Instead, they choose fields like law, medicine, and engineering—that command higher pay and often more respect. Today, I want to talk about how we can change this trend, transform the teaching profession, and ensure that the next generation of teachers is the very best we can offer our children.[4]

Because roughly half of America's 3.2 million active teachers could retire by the end of this decade, we have "an amazing chance to modernize the teaching profession and expand the talent pool," Duncan argues.[5] The primary change Duncan puts forth, designed to attract more "bright" and "committed" young people to teaching, is to change how much money teachers can make. "We should also be asking how the teaching profession might change if salaries started at $60,000 and rose to $150,000."[6] Duncan suggests:

> We should keep our best teachers in the classroom—and they should be earning a lot more money—as much as $150,000 per year. Let's face it: a phenomenal teacher educating underserved kids in science, technology, math, engineering, or the arts should be very well compensated—just as they are in other professions. A kindergarten teacher who can turn every child into a reader is priceless.[7]

We need to move away from "industrial-era blue-collar models of compensation" for teachers and move toward "rewarding effectiveness and performance."[8] Duncan goes on to say that "We have the incentives today all wrong—not just the money, but the prestige and the career opportunities." There is "an assembly-line model of pay, based on seniority and educational credentials," and with such blue-collar practices in place, we will never attract top college graduates.[9]

In order to pay (some) teachers the kind of money Duncan proposes we need to make significant changes in how we compensate teachers:

> We must ask and answer hard questions on topics that have been off limits in the past like staffing practices and school organization, benefits packages,

and job security—because the answers may give us more realistic ways to afford these new professional conditions.[10]

In this speech, Duncan does not say what kind of changes he would propose to these "off limits topics," but they are not hard to guess. Job security would involve getting rid of tenure and union-backed protective practices. Increases in teacher salary would have to be paid for by cuts in benefits packages and "staffing practices" that might involve greater student-to-teacher ratios or teachers taking on other institutional roles, perhaps administrative, in addition to their teaching duties. Some charter schools have adopted such practices so they can pay teachers more.

Duncan suggests other changes designed to attract the best and brightest to teaching. "Highly accomplished professionals" want autonomy—as would bright young people entering teaching—and in return they accept and even want to be held accountable for their performance.[11] Duncan applauds the National Board for supporting more rigorous teacher evaluation, including using student test scores to help weed out "a small minority of teachers who continue to struggle despite support and mentorship."[12] Standards of entry into the profession should be higher, he suggests, and he subtly accuses teacher education programs of being "cash cows" for universities, asserting they "lack the rigor to attract talented students."[13]

Secretary Duncan closes his remarks by saying he wants to work with teachers "to make teaching one of our nation's most venerated professions."[14] He notes that some "will hear the message about tradeoffs in terms of job security or benefits, and try to suppress the kind of open dialogue we need about the teaching profession." But, he says:

> I respectfully urge everyone to take a deep breath, hold their fire, and see this as an opportunity to transform the entire profession—not as a threat or as an investment we don't need. We respectfully need it. This isn't just coming from me—or some narrow segment of the reform community. This is coming from thousands of great teachers all across America who desperately want our respect, our support and our trust. This professional transformation won't happen unless teachers own this and drive this. Change can only come from the men and women who do the hard work every day in our classrooms.[15]

In his closing lines, Secretary Duncan urges the board certified teachers to lead the change effort:

> Bring their voice [the voices of colleagues] into the conversation, and help them see that by taking full responsibility for their profession, they can re-

make it in their own eyes—and in the eyes of our nation. And then we can all look forward to the day when people across society who meet a teacher come away with just one word on their lips: "Wow." Thank you.[16]

This speech to a very select audience does not, of course, mention other reform ideas championed by Secretary Duncan. He does not, for instance, mention changes to teaching demanded by *Race to the Top*—a $4.35 billion Department of Education program designed to spur reforms in state and local K–12 education.[17] Secretary Duncan is its chief architect and spokesperson. States competed for their piece of the 4.35 billion dollar pie by designing educational reforms according to strict criteria established by Department of Education officials. To qualify for funding, states had to make firm plans to do such things as improve teacher and principal effectiveness based on performance (especially standardized testing of students) and provide high-quality pathways for aspiring teachers and principals (find alternative ways to certify teachers and principals). They needed to embrace the adoption of Common Core State Standards and develop and implement common, high-quality assessments. They needed to agree to turn around and intervene in the lowest-achieving schools or shut them down, firing teachers and administrators. They also needed to show unambiguous support for creating high-performing charters and other innovative schools.

In his reform efforts, Secretary Duncan uses both warm and inviting rhetoric in his talks to teachers and the firm boot of educational policy in "incentivizing" change at state and local levels.

A Closer Look at Secretary Duncan's Remarks

Secretary Duncan says nothing in this speech that is overtly negative about teachers, save for noting (as anyone might do) that there are good teachers and bad teachers. There are no lines in his speech that teachers or others could single out as being outrageously offensive to teachers, and one can imagine that the speech was well received by the teachers in attendance at this event. Yet, despite Duncan's expression of admiration for the board certified teachers gathered for this event and his acknowledgment that there are great teachers working in classrooms, one doesn't get the sense that Duncan thinks much of teachers generally, taken as a whole. There is in his remarks an underlying tone that is less than complimentary toward today's teachers. And Duncan does, after all, argue for expanding the talent pool of teachers. One usually doesn't argue the need to expand an employment talent pool unless one believes the talent in the existing pool just isn't good enough.

Also, Duncan's speech has enough prickly comments about teachers to suggest he has grave reservations about many of them. Duncan seems to believe that most of today's teachers are highly protective of the status quo and are uninterested in putting themselves at risk in a remade profession. He never mentions teachers or teachers' unions as those who keep the hard questions of job security and other established practices "off limits," and neither does he name teachers as those who "try to suppress the kind of open dialogue we need about the teaching profession." However, one cannot read the whole of Duncan's speech and think he intends anyone else but teachers (and their unions) to be those most resistant to the changes he is proposing. Further, there is not enough of a "critical mass" of great teachers, Duncan says, and "There is a huge gulf of greatness and grit separating our best teachers from our worst."[18] Bright young people will bring the "grit"—the drive, the determination, the doggedness—we most need. And while no one can object to Duncan's call to "transform the teaching profession" so that we "ensure that the next generation of teachers is the very best we can offer our children," one sensitive to on-going criticisms of teachers cannot but hear in that statement a condemnation of the teachers teaching *this* generation of children. It seems we need better teachers in order to do a better job. That means those we have now aren't good enough.

At the close of his speech, Duncan speaks of the hope he has that one day teachers will be received with a sort of wide-eyed admiration, of the kind we now reserve for famous athletes: "Wow—you're a teacher." But, it appears from Duncan's remarks, teachers will not earn this respect the way they used to—on moral grounds, by dedicating their lives to the improvement of others with no expectation of great remuneration or professional prestige. Nor will they earn it by being called to serve others, by giving to others all that teachers have come to know and love. Instead, Duncan argues, teachers will earn admiration and respect only when they quit "suppressing" open dialogue, embrace a "new" profession, and accept the changes he sees as necessary—when they willingly agree to repeal tenure, give up collective bargaining, accept job performance evaluation based largely on student test scores, and support merit pay, etc. Then, and only then, will teachers receive the admiration and respect that we might want for them. Apparently, they won't deserve it until then.

Secretary Duncan and the Resentment of Teachers

There is nothing in Duncan's remarks, however, that looks and feels like the enflamed resentment and moral indignation of Jay P. Greene's condemnation of teachers examined in the previous chapter—nothing like the comparison of teachers to slave owners. In fact, Duncan makes a much more positive comparison—he wants teachers to be respected like doctors, lawyers, and other professionals. It would seem, then, that while Greene would perfectly fit the picture of "resentment" offered by Strawson in the last chapter, Secretary Duncan would not. Strawson, we recall, believes we respond with resentment and moral indignation when we believe we have been treated with indifferent disregard, outright contempt, or malevolence. Greene clearly believes teachers show such disregard and contempt and so deserve our resentment; Duncan says nothing of the kind.

We need to take a more careful look, however, and when we do, we cannot help but notice that both Greene and Duncan are looking at and criticizing the same thing—the self-interested attitudes of teachers. While these attitudes lead Greene to suggest the comparison to slaveholders, they lead Duncan to suggest why teachers don't yet deserve professional respect. Greene chooses a ghastly comparison he knows will alienate teachers, but he doesn't care. Duncan, on the other hand, is speaking to teachers and urging them to get their colleagues to accept the changes he proposes, so he chooses a very different rhetoric and a more conciliatory tone. But the message is essentially the same: the "education establishment," especially teachers, is firmly entrenched in self-interest. And until that self-interest is broken or redirected—that is, until teachers give up their current protections and show proper goodwill, affection, and esteem to students and the rest of us—our relationship with them will be strained, and they will need to be handled or managed with new policies. And Duncan, as Secretary of Education, is in the perfect place to direct those policies and bring teachers around.

If Duncan does not admit his resentment of teachers in this speech, he shows that he is out of patience with them, and there is probably only a fine line between the two. Duncan tells the enlightened teachers at the conference to work on their recalcitrant colleagues, those mired in a blue-collar vision of teaching centered on self-interest. He presents himself as on the side of the "thousands of great teachers all across America who desperately want our respect, our support and our trust." But he also insists on policies and new ways to manage, move, and shake the many more teachers who want to resist these changes. Duncan wants to resume his, and our, normal, good relationships with teachers—just as Strawson has proposed. But he is perfectly comfortable with an objective attitude that enforces policies and manages teachers. This he will do to bring teachers back to their proper care for us. And, of course, if these policies attract a better and brighter pool of talent into teaching, that's all the better.

Secretary Duncan would have room to disagree with this reading of the sub-text of his speech. His rhetorical ploys and careful word choice would give him "plausible deniability" to the charge that he does not respect teachers. Almost all state and federal legislators avail themselves of this same deniability. It is necessary to their political craft.

Pride and Vanity in Secretary Duncan's "Wow"

Every good speech, it seems, needs a good opening story or metaphor to set the mood and the intent on a given rhetorical occasion, and the rhetorical device Duncan chooses is the cartoon where a bunch of athletes want autographs from a teacher at a sports fantasy camp. The one athlete says of the teacher: "I wish I had that kind of money and respect." Duncan seizes on the incongruity of this image and comment, and he remarks: "We worship our athletes, our entertainers, our movie stars, but it is great teachers who really should trigger a "wow."

We can appreciate why Duncan would tell such a story. First of all, Duncan surely tells it in order to ingratiate himself to his audience, and the story certainly sets the stage for the argument that follows about the professionalization of teaching. And while Duncan certainly cannot expect people in our culture will "worship" teachers like we "worship" our most culturally prominent—our athletes, entertainers, and movie stars—Duncan surely wants teachers to be on par with other professionals who work in medicine, law, or other recognized professions. Money, respect, adoration, attention—the equal if not the envy of people in other professions—is what Duncan believes teachers want, and, as we have seen, he believes these will be the things that attract our best young people to teaching.

But the story Duncan tells—the guiding rhetorical device he chooses to make his argument for the professionalization of teaching—is poorly chosen. Beyond that, it is regrettable, especially when told by someone who stands, in some respect, as the leading representative of public school teachers. As a governing rhetorical device, the story illustrates in the clearest possible terms what it is that Secretary Duncan doesn't seem to understand or respect about teachers and teaching.

Pride and vanity are at the root of the cartoon about the balding teacher at the sports fantasy camp. Pride and vanity are the moral concepts embedded in the word "worship" as it is used in this story and as it is used in our popular culture. Vanity has to do with seeing yourself—and making sure others see you—as someone who deserves notice and attention. Vanity is a kind of command issued to others, a command that says "Drop what you're doing and notice *me.*" We easily recognize vanity in people we regularly adore—actors and actresses, sports figures, and the like. Part of their allure is their sense of themselves as deserving of and commanding our notice. We often resent pride and vanity in those immediately around us. Sometimes, we notice and regret it in ourselves, as well.

Secretary Duncan seems to accept pride and vanity unproblematically. He recognizes that people want to be noticed and appreciated for their skills and abilities—skills and abilities other people may not have. Duncan puts first in his new profession of teaching what he believes talented young people entering other professions (such as medicine or law) most want and demand: to command notice, respect, and admiration—in addition to an excellent salary. Vanity is a recruiting tool for Duncan, not a character flaw about which one should worry.

But I think vanity is misplaced in teachers. I don't think teachers naturally want or need to receive the same kind of attention and adoration that athletes, entertainers, or movie stars receive—and I don't think they want or need to receive the acclaim given to doctors, lawyers, or businessmen. Nor do I think we want them to. The "look at me" pride of central public figures (athletes, entertainers, and movie stars) is, after a while, usually seen as undeserved, hollow, and faintly pathetic; and it is seen that way, too, when it appears in doctors, lawyers, and other professionals. Pride and vanity—the need to be noticed and acclaimed—eventually wears thin on us all. And it seems particularly misplaced in service professions where the needs and interests of the professionals—of the teachers, nurses, or ministers—are often sacrificed, or minimized, in light of the needs and interests of those they serve. Vanity has no place in a service profession.

No teacher will turn down an increase in money or respect for the job he or she is doing, and every good teacher would like the good they are providing to be acknowledged. But this isn't vanity, or if it is, it is a mild sort of vanity—not the kind of vanity associated with the cultural or professional elite. This difference is important, and it goes unnoticed or unremarked by Secretary Duncan. Duncan just does not see the moral nature of teaching that is in every important respect antithetical to visible public acclaim.

What Secretary Duncan Doesn't Say to Teachers

Something is gone in the remarks of Secretary Duncan—something that used to be said when education leaders spoke of and to teachers. His effort to remodel teaching feels like an effort to remodel a room—a room where the old grandfather's clock, having stood watch on a family's life, generation after generation, is now lifted to the curb, no longer wanted. New things are now in the room—things some people surely like better than the old clock in the corner. But the room doesn't feel the same. Something essential is missing.

What is gone in Secretary Duncan's remarks are the ways we have always talked about teachers. Gone are the words we have always used to acknowledge the difficulties teachers face and our heartfelt appreciation for the efforts they make. Gone is the customary praise teachers have always liked to hear—not the words that bring public adoration, but the ones that bring modest satisfaction. Or, if those words are used, they seem to hold ghosts of ideas rather than genuine feelings. They seem more like necessary falsehoods one tells just to keep the peace, or like expressions of affection one offers just because one knows they are expected. They are like making a slight nod toward someone you really don't want to acknowledge, but have to. They seem like empty gestures.

In place of this old sincere language appears the language of professionalism and, very subtly, the language of resentment. Despite the demurrals of reformers, the scope and depth of the changes being proposed to teaching signal an abiding anger and resentment aimed at teachers. Duncan doesn't speak the old words to teachers partly because he prefers the language of professionalism—and partly because he doesn't think teachers really deserve the old words that always used to honor teachers. And he's not alone. Many people don't trust teachers anymore—they don't trust their skills and abilities, their demonstrated knowledge, their work ethic, the quality of care they show students, their motives, their passion, their effectiveness. The criticisms and reforms indicate the belief that teachers need to be managed, watched over, held accountable, and pressured to perform. And they need to be easily excised if found wanting. Bad teachers need to go, and more room needs to be made for other people likely to teach well.

Reformers, and many others, have lost faith in teachers.

Notes

1. Arne Duncan, "Working toward "Wow": A Vision for a New Teaching Profession" (Speech delivered to the National Board of Professional Teaching Standards, July 29, 2011), accessed October 25, 2014, *http://www.ed.gov/news/speeches/working-toward-wow-vision-new-teaching-profession*. See Appendix for full transcript.
2. Ibid., ¶2–3.
3. Ibid., ¶4.
4. Ibid., ¶5.

5. Ibid., ¶16.
6. Ibid., ¶21.
7. Ibid., ¶32.
8. Ibid., ¶21.
9. Ibid., ¶23.
10. Ibid., ¶21.
11. Ibid., ¶25.
12. Ibid., ¶10.
13. Ibid., ¶27.
14. Ibid., ¶32.
15. Ibid., ¶36.
16. Ibid., ¶37–38.
17. U.S. Department of Education, "Race to the Top," accessed October 25, 2014, http://www2.ed.gov/programs/racetothetop/index.html.
18. Duncan, *Working toward "Wow,"* ¶23.

4

Those Who Can't, Teach

Secretary Duncan's call to create a "new profession" of teaching with an "expanded talent pool" to include "bright" and "committed" young people is a complaint about the talents, abilities, and character of today's teachers and teacher education students. But we need to recognize that this complaint about teachers is not new—and it's certainly not just the opinion of Secretary Duncan or this particular batch of educational reformers. People have long worried about the skills, qualifications, and character of teachers.

Doers and Teachers

There is a nasty little phrase that comes up all too often when thinking or talking about teachers. You know the phrase: Those who can, do; those who can't, teach. This phrase is often attributed to H. L. Mencken, but seems to have appeared first in George Bernard Shaw's *Maxims for Revolutionists* (1903) attached to his play *Man and Superman.*[1] Taken as popular wisdom about teachers, this phrase captures another side of what many people

Blame Teachers, pages 43–56
Copyright © 2015 by Information Age Publishing
All rights of reproduction in any form reserved.

think about teachers and people who want to be teachers—first, that they are not smart or skilled enough to teach our children, and, second, that they lack ambition or *drive*.

The following bit of dialogue between two people is a common set-up for Shaw's classic "those who can't, teach" line. The imagined dialogue heightens the devastating critique of teachers:

> **Bob:** I'm so discouraged. My writing teacher told me my novel is hopeless.
>
> **Jane:** Don't listen to her, Bob. Remember: Those who can, do; those who can't, teach.[2]

Here, the response of the fictional Jane goes directly to the first criticism of teachers. Implicit in Jane's response is the idea that had the writing teacher been able to write, she wouldn't have been a writing teacher—she'd have been a novelist. The aspiring novelist, Bob—perhaps someone who really does have the skill, ability and drive to become a successful novelist—is taking writing lessons from a failure. This casts real doubt on the value of anything the teacher is teaching Bob. Her judgment of Bob's novel as being "hopeless" is especially in doubt. How is she to be trusted to make those kinds of judgments? How can she be trusted to teach anyone? Is she not more likely to ruin this potential novelist than help him?

Of course, this kind of logic makes anyone who teaches suspect. It suggests that anyone who teaches shouldn't be a teacher. Even if Bob's writing teacher had once been a successful novelist, she's still suspect. Why has she stepped away from writing novels and turned to teaching?

The phrase speaks to our worry about putting the education of the young in the hands of those understood to be less talented and able—those who have demonstrated they have less wit, intelligence, or skill than others. No personal or social good can be realized if the young are being educated and socialized ineptly. Why wouldn't we want our teachers to be the demonstrated best we have to offer? Does it not make some sense to think the best are those *doing* something in the field or discipline instead of those who are not or cannot? Why wouldn't we want our chemistry classes taught by a proven, practicing chemist, our choirs conducted by a working, proven singer, and our English composition classes taught by a published author?

But Shaw's phrase points beyond just a critique of the intelligence or skill of the teacher and touches an even more sensitive nerve, making the phrase as vitriolic and denigrating as a racist or ethnic slur. The phrase also demeans the character of teachers. Not only are teachers not as smart as people who enter the real world of doers, but they also lack the ambition, drive, or commitment of such people. Teachers are a full cut below others and need a softer, less competitive, less challenging, less demanding, and more protected work environment. They are unable to compete in the world of business and commerce and need the shelter of government work. They are "on the dole"—meaning they gain their sustenance from the goodness and largesse of tax-paying citizens. They are consumers of wealth, not producers of wealth. And they are this less because they choose to be rather than because they are incapable of much or anything else.

Resentment rests just behind (or inside) this "do and can't do" phrase. The person who is a doer in the world of business and commerce resents the laggard—the doer resents having to support or pay the way for others who he or she believes are not providing, and are not capable of providing, value. If doers believed that teachers were really providing an excellent education for the students in their charge—something, they would agree, was of real value—they would be less inclined to throw epithets in the direction of teachers. But they are not convinced, and so the assault on teachers continues.

Shaw's phrase neatly captures a whole host of worries about teachers. But, even more, the phrase captures the anger and resentment that many people have for teachers. The phrase holds and conveys the intensity and passion of someone who feels betrayed.

The Academic Performance of Teachers

But no matter how one feels about Shaw's little phrase, it appears there is some basis for it in fact. Critics of teachers (and teacher education programs) are only too happy to point these facts out.

Teacher education students, especially those seeking degrees in elementary education or early childhood education, do not, on average, have entering ACT or SAT scores as high as do their entering counterparts, especially those who seek degrees in the natural sciences.[3] Neither do graduating teacher education students typically score as high on the Graduate Record Examination (GRE) as do other graduating seniors.[4] The curriculum for teacher education students, especially elementary education majors and early childhood and family education majors, is thought soft and unworthy. Any kind of quick search of the internet on this subject reveals how people use these facts and understandings to castigate teachers, argue against pay raises for teachers, lobby for homeschooling, suggest that teacher education programs are awful and unnecessary, propose alternate routes to teacher certification—and more.

And then, of course, there are measures from international and national standardized tests, mentioned in the Introduction, that seem to confirm just how woeful our teachers and schools really are. Whether they use
TIMSS data that show our slipping position relative to other nations, or
state standardized tests that confirm our failing schools and school systems,
critics of teachers and the public schools have a mountain of data on which
to draw as they make their case against the quality of our nation's teachers.

That is not to say that all the indictments against teachers are true or
that all the facts used to buttress arguments about poor teacher quality are
as clear and unassailable as they may appear to be. The status of TIMSS
data or state standardized test scores as markers of educational quality is
constantly debated. It makes as much sense for critics of teachers to jump
from "look at these low test scores" straight to the conclusion "our teachers
are lousy" as it does for the businessman to jump from "look at my declin-
ing profits" to the conclusion "it's because my lousy workers are lazy and
overpaid." Complicated problems rarely parse out so conveniently.

And it's not that teachers and teacher educators are mute, or should
remain mute, in the face of this vituperative conversation. Teachers and
teacher educators have a legitimate response to Shaw's basic contention:
the ability of the doer (the chemist, the singer, or the novelist) to *do* his or
her discipline signals nothing about how well he or she might be able to
teach it. *Doing* a discipline and *doing teaching* of that discipline are two different things. The assassination of the teacher's character—that teachers
want or require "soft" working conditions because of some moral failure on
their part to embrace more aggressive values—has answer, as well.

But before we can defend teachers against the array of charges made
against them, we must finish the indictment. For it turns out critics make
more charges against teachers—charges, I'm afraid, that also have some
basis in fact and would seem to support Shaw's derisive phrase.

We have to look at why people become teachers.

Noble Reasons People Become Teachers

Any fair appraisal of why people become teachers will reveal both some noble
reasons and some less than noble reasons. We start with the noble reasons.

One reason people choose teaching comes out of our human desire
to want to live meaningful lives. We tend to know, deep down inside, that
we won't live fulfilling and meaningful lives if we care only about our own
needs and desires and never care about anyone else. Purpose and fulfill-

ment seem to require service to others, at least in part. That's one of the biggest reasons people become teachers—to serve others. The greatest reward of teaching comes from knowing you have done something to make the life of someone else better, deeper, richer, or easier. Teaching someone how to read and write, have basic competency with numbers, to know important things about the world, and to develop certain attitudes and appreciations—these are the acquisitions that give that person the tools to live happily and knowingly in the world. Not just to get a decent job and so be a "productive member of society," but to live a more interesting, involved and vibrant life.

Many people become teachers to pay a debt they believe they owe: some teacher in their past inspired them in a certain way, or cared for them at just the time they needed care, or counseled or supported them in some way. And now they want to do that for some other child. For other people, teaching is more of a call to duty; it is a way to address a lack of something, or a problem—to address social injustice, or moral turpitude, or a weakened sense of citizenship or patriotism, or even political, economic, or environmental problems. Others feel "called" to be a teacher not so much to be an agent of change, but in more of a spiritual or religious sense;[5] they feel called to give themselves over to what they understand as their life mission. Some want to serve the communities they grew up in. Some seem to be natural-born teachers—the child who "taught" the neighborhood kids when they played school, or the adolescent who discovered a knack for and enjoyment in explaining things to others.

But often there is something self-serving, too, that draws people to teaching—something, oddly enough, that is as noble a reason to teach as any other. Some people become teachers out of their love for a particular subject matter or discipline. They become teachers so they can continue to live with—to study, to enjoy, to think about and explore, and then to share—a field they love. They become teachers so they can help someone else love what they have loved. The American history teacher wants to teach American history partly because he loves to read and think about history—it helps him to understand himself, his country, other people, and current issues. He becomes a teacher because he wants to show his students how this study can be as meaningful to them as it is to him. It is the same for the music teacher who loves her music and the foreign language teacher who loves his language and culture. Each wants to spend time with what they love and immerse themselves more deeply in it.

There are, of course, reasons to worry about this motive for becoming a teacher. The teacher who sets aside the curriculum and the needs, desires, and abilities of students in favor of his or her personal exploration of a field or discipline is someone who has lost sight of his or her purpose. There are teachers who can drone on and on about some arcane aspect of subject matter, teaching way "above the heads" of students, and there are teachers who spend weeks and weeks going on about a favorite part of their field. Still, most of us remember as our best teachers those who loved their subject matter, knew it thoroughly, and could make it come alive. These teachers knew how to sweep us up in their love of the field, and this meant giving us the best and most interesting parts of it in ways we could understand and appreciate.

Less Than Noble Reasons People Choose Teaching

And now, some of the less noble reasons to become a teacher—even if we have to blush a little when we admit some of these. Probably, the most talked about of these less than noble reasons is that teachers get summers off. Mothers (mostly) but fathers, too, want to be on the same schedule as their children so family life can be more enjoyable and easier to manage. Day-to-day life is also easier to manage when children are school-age, and there are few evening obligations that take teachers away from their families at night.

While most people bemoan the low pay for teachers, many people entering teaching have quite a different impression. Teaching is still an "entry level" profession for members of many families—and to such people teaching looks distinctly better than available alternatives. The pay seems reasonable, especially given that teachers don't have to work 12 months to earn it. The work environment looks inviting, for the most part, and there is no travel or demanding physical labor involved with it. Fringe benefits are decent, especially health care benefits which are available not only for teachers but for their families. The retirement system for teachers has been both secure and adequate—better than adequate in some states.

Teaching has been a very secure job, too. Always, in the past, a teacher's paycheck has kept coming in, with the same dollar amount printed on it, even if the economy has taken a downturn. When school enrollments decline or budgets have to be trimmed during hard times, teachers can lose their jobs, but teachers have had more job security than most workers. Security is afforded, also, when teachers are awarded tenure. Contrary to what many believe, tenure is not a guarantee of lifetime employment, but it certainly allows teachers to anticipate continued employment. Especially for someone who wants to stay in the same place—because he or she wants to raise a family there, because of a spouse's job, because extended family lives there, or for a host of other reasons—the security offered by being awarded tenure in a school district has made a great deal of difference.

And now the part for which our Mr. Shaw would have been waiting.

Some people choose teaching by "default"—that is, they decide to become a teacher when some other plan falls through or is discarded. The student for whom medical school was once a hope and possibility gives up that idea (or has to give up that idea) and decides, instead, to become a biology teacher. The singer who pictured him or herself singing opera on Broadway learns he or she doesn't quite have the talent or drive to pull that off and decides to become a music teacher. Or the family business falls apart and the not-so-young man or woman decides to go back to school and earn a teaching certificate.

Some people choose teaching by default not because their high ambitions don't pan out (med school and opera on Broadway), but because they don't know what else to do. They have no great ambitions—maybe, not even a terrific grade point average—and it is time to pick something. Maybe mom and dad pressure them to "choose something and get on with it." And some people choose teaching just because they don't want to do something else—run the family business, work in a blue-collar job, exhaust themselves with physical labor, or something like that.

These last reasons for becoming a teacher would seem to concede Shaw's "those who can't, teach" position. Certainly, these aren't the most noble of reasons for choosing teaching. But we might note that just because something like these reasons move someone to choose teaching doesn't mean that person can't share in the more noble reasons discussed above. Just because med school didn't work out doesn't mean the teacher doesn't love biology and doesn't want to serve people. And just because someone struggles to choose a career, then chooses teaching, doesn't mean that person cannot love his or her field and become a wonderful teacher.

One final reason some people choose to become teachers: because they want to coach a sport's team. This becomes deeply problematic when classroom teaching is neglected or simply put up with so the coach can do what he or she really wants to do—coach his or her sport. This attitude has no place in schools. But when the teacher/coach uses his or her position to effect close and important relationships with both students and athletes, young people are rewarded. There is no doubt a teacher/coach can help students in considerable ways.

Career Choice is Complicated and Personal

I'm sure this little summary of the noble and not-so-noble reasons people choose teaching as a career has left something out. But surely this summary captures many of the reasons people make this choice—both the ones Shaw suspected and ones beyond his unsympathetic understanding of teachers.

But we've been painting this picture with a fairly wide brush, pointing to broad categories of reasons why people choose teaching as a career. We are not unjustified in doing so, but a real caution must be issued. We must remember that individuals make career decisions not with reference to any easy catalog of reasons, but because of their own particular circumstances. Factors that go into choosing a career are many, varied, and personal. A person may become a teacher—or a lawyer, a business owner, a salesman, a farmer, a mechanic, a homemaker, or anything else—for a host of different reasons: because of certain talents and abilities that appear relatively early in life that are either recognized and nurtured or neglected and unsupported; because of different family and community values and mores that shape the character of a person; because of the presence or absence of a family trade or business, or because of the education and social standing of parents; because of religious beliefs; because of judgments about what is realistic or possible given family and personal resources and one's history with learning in school; because of a preferred vision of one's future, especially one's economic future, and because of one's self confidence and sense of self-efficacy; because of the availability of certain post-high school education programs; and because of accidents, fate, happenstance and unforeseen life experiences. These factors, and more, mix and help determine one's career choice. It did for me—it does for all people.

What our Best College Graduates would Bring to Teaching

Some of the reasons people become teachers make them easy targets for those who are critical of teacher quality and want to reform the teaching corps—especially the default reasons listed above. Arne Duncan wants people who graduate from the top third of their college graduating class to become teachers—those, presumably, who have an array of attractive professional options from which to choose—not those who turn to teaching when a first or second option is eliminated. And he wants highly motivated people—people with grit, determination, and drive—not people with no great ambition, people who seem to slide into teaching because nothing else moves them. Those who choose teaching for the security it has offered—for the reasonable pay and benefits and for the opportunity to live and stay in a particular community—are a little suspect, too. Job security is seen as a blue-collar virtue, and choosing a career for family, home and community reasons is more maternal than professional.

On the face of it, Duncan's argument makes sense. Choosing more teachers from the top third of college graduates is decidedly better than choosing more teachers from the bottom two thirds, especially from the bottom third, to the extent that is happening. We all might agree that it is better to have a bright, energetic, committed young person choose teaching—someone who has actively chosen teaching from a variety of equally or more attractive career possibilities—than someone who backs into teaching when other career doors are slammed in his or her face, or when someone chooses teaching only because it provides security or convenience for oneself or one's family.

The object for Duncan, we remember, is to remake the teaching profession—to bring to teaching a new quality of person he believes will neither need nor want any of the existing conditions of teaching, things like tenure, pay schedules, unionism, or weak teacher evaluation. This is the better, stronger college graduate. System change depends on getting these top students into teaching, and when the system finally changes, problems in education will be made better. All the blue-collar courtesies of teachers that protect inept teachers will be eliminated, and those who thrive in a competitive merit-based environment—those who don't mind tough standards and being held accountable for reaching them—will be turned loose. And students will benefit. And our schools will improve.

Teach for America: The Best of the Best

This is certainly the argument made by Wendy Kopp, founder of Teach for America and a central figure in educational reform. Educational reformers often point to Teach For America as an example of what it would be like if we chose more bright, energetic people to be teachers from the top third of college graduating classes. The Teach For America program recruits college graduates from among our best colleges and universities. Very few students recruited into the program have any intention of becoming teachers when they enter college, and so almost none of them take teacher education classes while in school. After they graduate, TFA offers their recruits a five week summer training to prepare them to teach disadvantaged students in underserved neighborhoods, rural or urban, all across the nation. These members of the TFA "corps" agree to teach in these areas for at least two years. They are compensated like other beginning teachers are compensated—with full salary and comprehensive benefits—but they receive many other benefits not available to other beginning teachers including AmeriCorps benefits of $11,290 if they successfully complete their two years of service.[6]

The object is to lure top students into teaching—not just the top third of college graduates that Duncan talks about, but the top graduates from our *best* colleges and universities, places like Harvard, Cornell, or Princeton, which claim among their graduates, respectively, Arne Duncan, Michelle Rhee, and Wendy Kopp. These are the people who have the intelligence and drive to help our most disadvantaged students make "life-transforming" change. In her book *A Chance to Make History: What Works and What Doesn't in Providing an Excellent Education for All,* Wendy Kopp writes,

> We will need to rally the country to embrace a new mandate for urban and rural public schools—to provide transformational education. We must build within schools in economically disadvantaged communities the mission and capacity not simply to make learning opportunities available but to ensure that children actually master the skills, knowledge, and habits of mind that set them up to have a full set of life options and that ultimately put them on a different path than the one predicted by their socioeconomic background.[7]

Little of what educators have tried in the past, according to Kopp, has "moved the needle against the achievement gap that persists along racial and socioeconomic lines."[8] That's because we haven't had what we most need, what Kopp repeatedly calls "transformational leadership." Transformational leaders, be they teachers, principals, or people who open schools, are "individuals who believe deeply in their students, who invest them and their families in an ambitious vision of success, and who do whatever it takes to get there." The mission of Teach For America, according to Kopp, "is to be one source of this transformational leadership."[9]

Teach for America intends not just to serve students in disadvantaged areas through the teaching of corps members—it intends to "push the frontier of education reform today" and to "effect change on a larger scale."[10] A TFA alumnus, Kopp reports, sponsored legislation in Colorado that, among other things, tied tenure and teacher evaluation to the academic progress of students and ended "last hired, first fired" practices.[11] Others have opened schools or, like Michelle Rhee, gained powerful educational posts. This kind of transformational leadership requires the intellect and energy of our best college graduates—not usually those who have gone through typical teacher education programs in a more average college or university.

The live minds of TFA corps members are idealistic and open to new and challenging ideas; corps members haven't been soured by the pessimism and failed ideas of the past. Kopp reports that her eight year old child once asked her "how if this is such a big problem—you know, kids not having the chance to have a good education—why would you ask people with no experience right out of college to solve it?" Kopp's answer:

> I started by sharing my view that although it's true that experience can be invaluable, there's also a power in inexperience—that it can make a huge difference to channel the energy of young people, before they know what's "impossible" and when they still have endless energy, against a problem that many have long since given up on. They can set and meet goals that seem impossible to others who know more about how the world works.[12]

What we most need, Kopp asserts, is what we haven't had—a "talent mind-set." She cites Jim Collins, author of *Good to Great*, who offered what is, I think, an unfortunate analogy about talent when applied to educating the underserved. Collins' studies of organizations, Kopp reports, revealed that

> . . . those [organizations] that rose above the crowd and became great were the ones that "got the right people on the bus, the wrong people off the bus, and then the right people in the right seats."[13]

If we follow the analogy Kopp finds useful, then we conclude that average teachers and average administrators trained in average teacher education programs have been driving the bus for too long. We can criticize these educators for failing to "move the needle" against the achievement gap, but, even more, we can indict them for a failure of character and commitment. They have not truly believed in their students, nor provided them with a vision of success, nor done "whatever it takes" to ensure students are successful. Not only do such people need to stop driving the bus, they need to be kicked to the curb. Programs like Teach For America will supply us with the kinds of transformational teachers and administrators we need.

How Teachers Hear Talk about Professionalism

One thing is clear from the kind of educational critique offered by Kopp: our current generation of teachers and administrators, taken as a whole, as well as those who have come before them, aren't getting credit for much of anything. Nothing about the results they have achieved is notable, and nothing about their aptitude and character is right—not their intellect, not their vision, not their drive, not their commitment, and not their reasons for wanting to teach. If Kopp is right, those we have been hiring as teachers are precisely the ones who *can't*; now we need to hire the ones who *can*. Kopp shows no respect, no goodwill, and no affection for "typical" public school teachers prepared in the usual ways. Teachers understand this very clearly. Both teachers and teacher educators can recognize an insult when they hear one.

But Kopp's is not an isolated voice. Kopp, Duncan and many others insert the language and ideas of *professionalism* and *transformational leadership* where a very different language and set of ideas about teaching has always existed. This new language speaks of prestige, pay, "human capital," change, "pushing the frontier of education reform," drive, ambition, and power. It is an aggressive language, an aggressive professional vision of teachers. It isn't a language that cancels the noble reasons for teaching mentioned above, even though those reasons may sit uneasily in this new vision. But it most certainly is a language that wants to cancel many, if not all, of the "not so noble" reasons people have entered teaching. *Stability, security, pension*, and *salary schedule*—these are words that signal failing teachers and failed teaching, and, according to Kopp, Duncan and others, these words are poisonous. Aggressive words—*drive, ambition, power*—reflect the new view of teachers and a necessary road to the remaking of teaching.

This change in language about teaching is noticeable and bothersome to those accustomed to using a different language to think about themselves and what they do. This language seems to come at the expense of more established ways of talking about teaching. This is, in part, what I was alluding to at the end of Chapter 3 in commenting on the empty and unsatisfying way Secretary of Education Duncan talks about teachers and teaching.

Here is what Duncan and others don't seem to acknowledge. We used to honor teachers precisely for what does *not* come with the kind of profession or professionalism Duncan desires for teachers and teaching. We have honored teachers, in part, because they seem to worry about things above and beyond prestige, acclaim, money, and power—even "profession." We assumed people chose teaching for the noble reasons catalogued above, even if they weren't always the top students in their college class and even if they also wanted security and stability in their lives. Yet, the remarks of Duncan and so many other educational reformers seem to dismiss all this. Muted in the remarks of Duncan, Kopp, and others are words that want to honor today's teachers for their selfless dedication, for heeding the call to teach, for committing themselves to worthy ends like social justice, the environment, or even love of subject matter. Gone is an appreciation for teachers working for modest pay, rooting themselves in a community, soldiering on when communities refuse even modest tax increases to support their schools. Gone is an appreciation for the reasons someone might pick an occupation based in part on considerations of family, or community, or stability. Gone is an acknowledgement that people want to be teachers because they want to be important in small, quiet, and private ways.

If reformers and legislators valued security and stability for teachers the way teachers have always valued these things, they wouldn't strip away tenure, the traditional salary schedule, and retirement benefits. If they valued the quiet modesty of a wonderful teacher—someone not inclined to boast about her successes with students—they wouldn't make her prove her value, especially in superficial ways, through comparison to the performance of her peers. If they believed teachers could think through their subject matter capably and could pose it to students the way students need it, they wouldn't standardize every aspect of the curriculum. If they valued the unspoken, personal, and mostly noble reasons that move people to become teachers, they wouldn't remake teaching for people who require money and prestige. Or, they wouldn't think that only the best graduates, mostly from our elite colleges and universities, were capable of becoming excellent teachers.

Maybe reformers have good reason to challenge established values and practices. No doubt it is, indeed, time to upset some of them. But clearly educational reformers, legislators, and many others don't want to sing the old noble hymns about the virtues of America's teachers. In place of these hymns is a confident language about the necessity of change, of "transformational change," a language that asserts the virtues of leadership and professionalism. Placed alongside the modest, always morally tinged language we have always used to talk about the practice of teaching and the passions of our teachers, the language of professionalism and change seems loud, abrasive, and more than a little self-congratulatory. It isn't a language heard easily or welcomed by teachers who have grown-up with and been moved by the older, simpler, and more modest language that seemed to describe how and why they wanted to be teachers and what their teaching practice was all about.

Educational reformers, legislators, businessmen, and others who speak the new language are, for teachers, a little suspect—especially if, like Duncan, Rhee, and Kopp, they have no, or very little, direct teaching experience. The self-congratulatory tone of reformers smacks of hubris—that excess of pride that, for the ancient Greeks, was necessary for the greatest heroes, but totally misplaced, and fatal, in those pretenders to greatness. And if those within the range of the reformer's remarks, especially teachers (and teacher educators) for whom those remarks are mostly intended, believe they hear hubris, they'll also hear condescension. The one often comes with the other. The man plainly and outwardly convinced of the superiority of his vision gets no hearing from an audience convinced of his condescending tone.

Notes

1. George Bernard Shaw, "Maxims for Revolutionists," *Bernard Shaw: Complete Plays with Prefaces* (New York, NY: Dodd, Mead & Company, 1962), 733. Mencken would have only been 23 years old when the play was written, and so the attribution to Shaw. The exact quote from Shaw is "He who can, does. He who cannot, teaches."
2. "Those who can, do," *McGraw-Hill Dictionary of American Idiom and Phrasal Verbs* (New York, NY: The McGraw-Hill Companies, 2002).
3. "2012 College-Bound Seniors Total Group Profile Report (PDF)," accessed October 25, 2014, http://media.collegeboard.com/digitalServices/pdf/research/TotalGroup-2012.pdf.
4. "GRE Guide to the Use of Scores (PDF)," accessed October 25, 2014, www.ets.org/gre/institutions/scores/interpret/.
5. David Hansen, *The Call to Teach* (New York, NY: Teachers College Press, 1995).
6. "Compensation and Benefits," accessed October 25, 2014, http://www.teachforamerica.org/why-teach-for-america/compensation-and-benefits.
   TFA corps members can use this money to repay student loans they incurred during their undergraduate study or they can spend it on advanced degrees. A number of colleges and universities will match this money for TFA corps members. In addition, corps members can postpone regular monthly loan payments during their two-year commitment, and AmeriCorps will pay all interest that accrues on qualified student loans while these people are in the corps. Corp members may also apply for need-based transitional loans and grants to help them with some of their expenses.
7. Wendy Kopp, *A Chance to Make History: What Works and What Doesn't in Providing an Excellent Education for All* (New York, NY: Public Affairs, 2011), 9.
8. Ibid., 6.
9. Ibid., 11.
10. Ibid., 184–185.
11. Ibid., 161.
12. Ibid., 177–178.
13. Ibid., 149. Quoted from Jim Collins, *Good to Great: Why Some Companies Make the Leap . . . and Others Don't* (New York, NY: HarperBusiness, 2001), 13,1.

5

Standards, Accountability, and the Value of Learning

In many respects, reformers who are frustrated with teachers are like parents who are frustrated with their misbehaving or disobedient teenager. When faced with what they take to be an intolerable situation, both parents and reformers believe themselves in need of a policy—something new that will correct the problem. The frustrated parent might choose to communicate the newly chosen policy to the teenager using "either/or" language. We can imagine, for instance, the parent saying something like this to a curfew-missing teenager: "Either you figure out a way to get home by midnight, or you can forget about driving the car for a while." This kind of either/or statement describes both a condition and a consequence—a policy, a plan—the kind of policy we adopt when we are taking an objective attitude toward someone who needs to be steered toward showing us the esteem and goodwill we believe we deserve. Following what we learned from our Chapter 2 detour into the work of P. F. Strawson, we can be sure that when such policies are issued, emotions are riding pretty high and blame and resentment are at hand.

Blame Teachers, pages 57–75

57

Reformers do not apologize for the iron-fisted, no-nonsense/no excuses policies they seek to enact. At the heart of most of these policies is something like an either/or alternative aimed at teachers. At its crudest, the message is "Either improve your performance, or look for another job." But this way of putting the message casts educational reform policies in the harshest of lights. And while critics like Jay P. Greene may only require this kind of light, others like Arne Duncan want to argue for a softer, more productive light—a velvet return, if you will, to the iron-fist of reform policies.

Both the frustrated reformer and the concerned parent want something more than sheer obedience to the policies they enact. The frustrated parent wants something more than a spiteful glare as the teenager splashes the keys down at 11:59 every time he or she comes home. And reformers like Arne Duncan want something more than resentful teachers grimly churning through curriculum to prepare students for the next standardized test. Duncan wants these reforms to rekindle something for teachers—an interest, a spark, a commitment. He wants energy and excitement, and he wants revitalized school communities. Both parents and reformers want those subjected to new policies to see the wisdom of those policies—to agree that they are best, to embrace them cheerfully. The parent wants the teenager to resolve his or her indifferent disregard or contempt for the parent—that disregard and contempt revealed by his or her habit of returning home well after midnight. Reform policies are supposed to get teachers to do the same thing—to resolve their indifferent disregard or contempt for students and the community. Like the cheerful midnight return of the teenager signals his or her renewed affection for parents, the energy, new dedication, and improved performance of teachers will signal their return to the proper relationship with students and the community—one characterized by affection, esteem, and goodwill.

Those of us who have been around resentful teenagers know, however, that this might be a little easier said than done. And it also might be true that the new policies reformers have set for teachers—especially those having to do with standards and teacher evaluation—bring some problems and limitations to teaching and learning that reformers don't quite see.

Standards and Accountability

We noted in Chapter 1 that reformers like Duncan, Greene, and Kopp do not have the technical expertise to tell teachers *how* they should teach or what they should be doing differently in the classroom. But that doesn't mean there aren't other mechanisms in place that change teaching and learning in classrooms. We also noted in Chapter 1 that reforms quite deliberately center on a teacher's core responsibility—to see that students have learned what has been identified for them to learn. This started happening in the late 1980s and early 1990s when, with the publication of *A Nation at Risk* and similar books, the standards and accountability movement gained fresh momentum. In 2001, the No Child Left Behind Act (NCLB) brought standards and accountability squarely in the middle of the conversation about schools. With standards made clear and accountability taken seriously, teachers had no choice but to take notice and change their teaching and curriculum. Now, the new centerpiece of standards and accountability are the Common Core State Standards, and standards and accountability measures drench every aspect of school curriculum and general school life. There is hardly a breath taken in most public school classrooms that isn't filled with some curricular standard or some worry about how students will demonstrate mastery of that standard.

Why Standards and Accountability Make Sense to Us

Most of us tend to view standards in a positive light—not just education standards, but standards pertaining to all manner of different things from automobile safety, to food quality, to building requirements. One function of standards is to express, in clear terms, what will be accepted as a minimum level of quality or performance in a given area. That is, standards draw the line between what is acceptable and what is unacceptable. Sometimes, this drawing of the line has the actual power of law behind it, as in the case of automobile safety with all the sanctions and penalties that go with a violation of an expressed standard. For schools and school districts, sanctions and penalties may include funding cuts or loss of accreditation. Now, for teachers, failure to meet standards can result in getting fired. Wherever we find them, standards always express the toughness or sternness of unyielding expectations. They also suggest two very different roles—that of the watcher and the one watched. Some people are going to judge things, or judge people, and others are going to be judged.

We erect standards for our own protection, and standards are to have a kind of "everyness" quality to them. This means two things—first, that *every* person, product, act, or event that is subject to standards must live-up to those standards—for instance, that *every* car rolling off the assembly line will meet *every* standard set for it; and, second, that *everyone* is to be protected by these standards. Standards are inclusive. They are supposed to be sensible and reasonable, and they are supposed to catch everything for everybody. If some product or act somehow slips through and doesn't meet the standard erected for it—or if individuals or groups of people do not meet the standards erected for them—we are justified in feeling betrayed, bamboozled, or, at the very least, let down. We are especially betrayed and angry when we find out that people have actively ignored or circumvented the standards and procedures put into place to protect people. General Motors learned this the hard way in spring and summer 2014 when their flagrant violation and cover-up of numerous safety standards was exposed. We feel betrayed and angry when we discover that some teacher, or some school, has been ducking standards and offering students a substandard education.

Of course, with everyness comes sameness: because every given product has to meet the same rigid standard as every other product of that type, they all start looking the same. Most of the time, that's just fine. For example, we all want the same excellent protection that comes with infant car seats, and we don't care if all car seats have the same basic features or look the same. We make the same argument about subject classes or grade-level classes in schools. State standards are intended to make sure, for instance, that all Algebra I students, or all third grade students, have learned the same things and have the same skills once they have completed the course, no matter where they went to school or which teacher they had. We know the reason this is important—to protect every math student, or every third grader, from getting something far less than what they deserve. Education standards are intended to prevent what was not prevented at GM. General Motors produced cars—just not cars that worked very well. Schools and teachers are supposed to graduate students who work well—who are "career or college ready." Every student in every teacher's classroom is expected to do everything specified in a particular set of standards. That's a sameness thought desirable.

This "sameness" is a little tricky, of course. First of all, children aren't automobiles or car seats, and an Algebra I or third grade classroom isn't a manufacturing center. (And Algebra and third grade teachers aren't all like the set of GM executives who apparently didn't care if their cars weren't safe and who worked to cover up their ineptness.) The sameness that comes with standards is very problematic when it comes to the real students and teachers who populate classrooms. But, many would argue, the sameness that comes with meeting teaching and learning standards does not prohibit uniqueness in classrooms any more than it prohibits uniqueness in automobiles. For instance, both a Ford Focus and a Lexus GS meet the same standards set for automobiles, be they safety standards, or mileage standards, or whatever. But they are still very different cars. Why couldn't third grade teachers or Algebra I teachers create different and unique classes and learning environments even as they and their students meet all designated standards? Standards don't kill creativity and inventiveness, many argue—they merely establish a baseline for what is acceptable.

Finally, we like to view standards through an even more optimistic lens. Standards help us realize our better selves. They encourage us to do what we are capable of doing. We know we are doing the right thing when we "hold ourselves to a higher standard," or when someone else holds us to that higher standard. What we had been doing might have been "good enough," but we are capable of something better. "Good is the enemy of great," says Jim Collins, a favorite of Wendy Kopp's.[1] And great is certainly what we want from teachers—and it's what students deserve. Education standards articulate goals as they press teachers to reach them. Standards help both teachers and students realize their potential. This is an understanding of standards embraced not just by educational reformers, but by state education officials, teachers, school administrators, and teacher educators as well.

The sense of teacher accountability that goes alongside this vision is likewise natural enough for many of these same people to support. If we are serious about standards, we have to insist people (or things) meet those standards. And that means we have to check, and judge, and insist on consequences if standards are not met. End-of-the year standardized tests, we might agree, don't tell us everything about teaching and learning in classrooms as clearly and absolutely as would a failed safety, or fuel mileage, or emissions test for automobiles; but many see student test scores as our best approximation to some valid, reliable, and presumably fair measure of whether or not teachers are effective. These tests give us a basis for comparing teachers—one Algebra teacher with all the other Algebra teachers, one third grade teacher with all the other third grade teachers—and they give us a basis for comparing schools. This data gives those who play the role of judge or decision-maker a basis for holding teachers and schools "accountable" by imposing sanctions or firing teachers when scores don't measure-up to expected or mandated standards. Standards without teeth mean nothing.

How Teaching Changes Under the Guardianship of Standards and Accountability

Teachers have known since the NCLB days that there are some very critical and potentially devastating consequences for schools, and for themselves, if standardized test scores don't go up. This has been made patently clear to teachers by the lecture/scolding/encouragement/threat/pep talk they have received from the district superintendent or school principal at the beginning of every school year. NCLB proponents may have hoped teachers and school administrators would respond to this testing pressure by talking about improving the depth and quality of learning for all students. And proponents certainly had some expectation that increased test scores would be some indicator of improved depth and quality of learning.

But when there is so much riding on making sure that test scores go up, teachers and school administrators are not first going to talk about depth and quality of learning. They're going to talk about test scores. Under the direction of school administrators in the NCLB days, teachers quite naturally talked about getting to the next required percentage level in order to make AYP, or Adequate Yearly Progress. They talked about—and were *forced* to talk about—scouring last year's test data to identify the 20 or 30 students who, on the last state test, weren't quite at the proficient level or who had just barely scored at that level. The talk was about how teachers could help those students so they would score at the proficient level on the next state test, this so the school wouldn't receive NCLB sanctions. That *is* a conversation about student learning; and to the extent those standardized tests forced teachers to make an extra effort with particular students to ensure those students learned important material or skills—and to the extent that the tests forced teachers to tend to curriculum matters more closely—then the tests had some value. In the name of *accountability*, these tests forced teachers to take care that students were not slipping through the cracks.

When Standards Become a Teaching Contract

When Common Core State Standards, NCLB test standards, or state curriculum standards get winnowed down and organized as learning outcomes in curriculum guides put together by local school districts, they become terms of a contract—a contract that stipulates that, by the end of the year or semester, the teacher *will teach*, and the teacher will make sure that students *will learn*, what is listed in the curriculum guide. Standardized tests make sure this gets done, and so do textbooks and other curricular materials built around the standards. Teachers get a clear message from all this: teach what you're supposed to teach—teach what's on the list. They are very often told to list the particular objective(s) or learning goal(s) for the day on the board not just so students will know, but so that teachers will not forget and so wandering administrators can be assured that learning is on-task—or "on-standards." Teachers talk together about how the curriculum must be arranged so that all the standards and learning objectives can be met by the end of the year.

The thinking behind this standards-based approach is not silly. A tenth grade geometry teacher is supposed to teach geometry, and teach it seriously and thoroughly, just like a fourth grade teacher is supposed to teach all the parts of his or her curriculum, and in the same way—that is, seriously and thoroughly. Each curriculum can be clarified, broken down, listed—in fact, curriculum seems to demand that it be separated out into distinct topics, ideas, units, skills, knowledge, or understandings. A geometry teacher who doesn't tend carefully to teaching about right angles, or congruent angles, or the Pythagorean theorem—and who doesn't make sure students have secure understandings of these things—will have failed as a teacher just as surely as the fourth grade teacher who doesn't teach percentages, or multiplying fractions, or whatever else his or her curriculum demands. Standards clarify the curricular contract, and standardized tests assess whether or not the contract has been fulfilled. This makes it possible to argue that a teacher driven to make students know and understand all identified standards or objectives—even if only so that students will score well on the state test and so make the teacher look good—is still being an effective teacher. Pressure put on teachers results in student learning, and that's all that matters.

A clear curricular contract also encourages a method of "managing" and evaluating teachers beyond the key final result of the year-end standardized test. The tenth grade geometry teacher has always been expected to find out, upon his teaching of the Pythagorean theorem, whether or not his students know and understand the concept. That is, the teacher has always been expected to devise some assessment of student learning and to engage in some re-teaching if the assessment indicates students are still confused. But in a standards- and accountability-centric educational environment, all aspects of that particular piece of the curriculum—or any and all other pieces—can get heightened scrutiny. Wendy Kopp suggests that leaders in the most successful schools, especially the KIPP (Knowledge is Power Program) schools with which she is most familiar, manage teachers very carefully at this smaller level. Each teacher has weekly one-on-one meetings with his or her "manager" where the teacher's progress toward various performance goals is assessed or where weekly progress assessments of student performance are examined.[2] Such sessions are informed by data about student learning, and Kopp wants more academic assessments, not fewer—assessments that are deeper, more rigorous, and more thorough.[3] These assessments and the weekly meetings with managers are conducted "in the spirit of ensuring that every teacher is leading students to fulfill their potential" and to ensure that everyone is meeting the standards expected of them.[4] That is, we might say, the meetings intend to find out if the teacher is meeting the terms of his or her implied contract to make sure students are learning designated material. This management approach centered on assessing whether or not a teacher has attained particular and limited goals isn't used just in charter schools that Kopp and others admire so much. It's being used in other "regular" public schools, too.

There is much that can and needs to be said about this approach to managing teachers and making sure that teachers manage their teaching in such ways. The first is to note how strange and uncomfortable it is, for many people, to hear talk of "managing teachers." Certainly, the history of education in America is replete with examples of how leaders have tried to control curriculum and control teachers, from the creation of "the one best system" until now.[5] Public school teachers have never been, nor should they be, free agents to do whatever it is they want to do in the classroom. But teachers have usually enjoyed a kind of latitude in the conduct of their teaching—a professional discretion or professional trust—that gets diminished or eradicated when their relationship with superiors is conceived using the language of management. *Managers* work in restaurants and clothing stores at the mall or in large corporate environments—and *management* is the language of the relationship between employers and workers. Management is a language often used to distinguish power and control, a language that separates *superiors* from *underlings*. It is not the language usually employed to describe the relationship between principals (or instructional leaders) and teachers, until now.

There is, furthermore, a kind of disconnect between Kopp's use of the language of management and the kind of profession and professional teacher for whom Arne Duncan longs. Duncan wants to attract the top college graduate into teaching—the kind of person who now becomes a doctor, lawyer, or engineer because teaching lacks pay, prestige, and professional working conditions. But does the kind of data-driven intense watchfulness of employee production suggested by Kopp sound like an attractive professional environment in which to work? Would someone who could be a doctor or lawyer opt for an environment where they are to be so closely "managed" and where professional discretion and trust is minimized?

The language of *management* again signals the doubt, mistrust, blame, and resentment that lie behind so many of the ideas and plans of educational reformers and persuaded policy-makers. Absent that doubt and mistrust, and absent the objective attitude that characterizes so many of their policies, many of the actual reform ideas have significant merit. There is nothing wrong with clarifying intended student learning with standards or grade and course level expectations. The need to get students to master a goal or standard can get teachers to respond to students who are struggling instead of merely recording their failure in a grade book. Neither is there anything wrong with tests or other measures of student learning that can both further student learning and identify possible weaknesses or lapses in a teacher's teaching. As we saw above, reformers can justify these and other changes on pretty solid ground—a moral ground having to do with making sure we're doing the best we can for students, and a perfectly legitimate pedagogical ground that most educators acknowledge, and many educators embrace fervently.

But the doubt and mistrust—the blame, resentment, and objective attitude that informs and motivates these changes—changes everything for most teachers. With a clearly perceived doubt and mistrust, standards and expectations aren't standards and expectations—they're an imperative that comes with an implied threat, a "Do this—or else." Tests aren't helpful pedagogical devices designed to assist student learning—they are traps for teachers, a "Gotcha!!" waiting to happen. Neither are the tests there to help teachers improve their practice but to punish them if they don't perform up to expectations. And discrete curricular standards or learning objectives aren't helpful ways to break down the curriculum into manageable parts— they become the fine print of the teaching contract, the every-little-detail that must be manically attended to if the teacher isn't going to have to face his or her disapproving manager. And we know of some regrettable or even nightmarish teaching practices that come with standards and accountability when the pressure on teachers is ratcheted up—when teachers engage in weeks of test preparation less oriented to mastering the subject than to mastering how to take the state test;[6] or when standards and objectives can be like items on a list you take to the grocery store—just pick the item up, cross it off the list, and move on to the next aisle.

Standards almost always create boundaries to the thinking of teachers and administrators—places to stop thinking about what they are doing and why they are doing it. There is always an implied message in standards that says "We've done your thinking for you—just do this." Standards are more than expectations, even when accountability measures like standardized tests are not tied to them. They always imply an impending judgment— an "either you measure-up or you don't"—that pushes teachers into compliance with them. And when critical accountability measures get directly linked to those standards with standardized testing—when schools can close and teachers can lose their jobs if scores aren't high enough—standards become the be-all and end-all for schools.

New Teacher Evaluation Systems

Standards and accountability thinking motivated by doubt and mistrust of teachers gets formalized in new teacher evaluation systems. Many of these new systems use value-added assessments of teachers and other calculations of student performance on standardized tests to determine the effectiveness of teachers—these measures sometimes counting for up to half of a teacher's evaluation "score." Tennessee's evaluation system is called TEAM—the Tennessee Educator Acceleration Model (TEAM). In that model 35% of a teacher's evaluation is calculated using the Tennessee Value-Added Assessment System (TVAAS) with an additional 15% of the evaluation coming from other measures of student achievement. The TVAAS value-added statistical model compares each student's end-of-the-year score on a standardized test to a battery of previous scores calculated to determine each student's expected score.[7] Teachers whose students score above this expected score have *added more value* to students than teachers whose students score below their expected scores. Teachers in Washington D.C. are evaluated with a similar system called IMPACT where 35% of a teacher's evaluation is determined from value-added measures and 15% from other student achievement data.[8] Both Washington D.C. and Tennessee also use classroom observations and conferences in evaluating teachers. Forty percent of a teacher's total evaluation score is derived from these observations and conferences in D.C. and 50% in Tennessee. In D.C., a Teaching and Learning Framework is used to score the teacher's effectiveness during classroom observations. This framework emphasizes the need for teachers to organize their year in accord with district content standards and teach lessons that are "objective-driven."

Numbers are also important in Missouri's new teacher evaluation program (Missouri's Educator Evaluation System) even though it does not use value-added measures.[9] The key annual evaluation process involves the teacher consulting with his or her principal or other designated instructional leader to find three "indicators" to work on for that year. School priorities, troubling results from last year's standardized tests, or perceived weaknesses or needs the teacher may have will determine which indicators that teacher is to work on during the year. Each teacher gets scored on the three chosen indicators—first, with an initial or "baseline" score near the beginning of the school year and then with a "post-test" score at the end of the year after a year-long professional growth plan developed around these three indicators has been implemented. In this system, a teacher is given a score from 1–7 on each of the chosen indicators. A score of one indicates an emerging but inconsistent skill for the teacher, and a seven indicates consistent "distinguished" performance.

Evaluators are looking for "growth" in these designated areas. In an initial draft of the plan, the scores on the three indicators taken at the beginning of the year were to be added together and divided by three, yielding a "baseline" number for the teacher's evaluation. After receiving professional development aligned to the three chosen indicators, the three post-test numbers were also to be added together and divided by three. The "growth score" would be determined by subtracting the baseline number from the post-test number. In the current version of the plan, growth scores are raw numbers—hopefully, numbers that show improvement. A teacher who improves from a three to a five during the course of the year on one indicator, would, for instance, show a "Growth score" of two on that indicator. A failure to show growth on an indicator would be cause for alarm.

Teacher evaluation policies such as the ones in Missouri, Tennessee, and Washington D.C. are the natural consequence of standards and accountability thinking that has taken over the schools. We require proof that teachers are meeting the standards set for them. Data mined from value-added statistical models and raw numbers from student performance on standardized tests provide what is understood to be a reliable and valid assessment of teacher performance. The complicated statistical methodologies involved with value-added analyses force us to trust statisticians a bit more than we feel comfortable doing, but the attempt to measure the real result of what students have learned against what they were expected to learn has some appeal. We very likely would learn something important if the students of one teacher consistently exceed expectations while students of another teacher consistently fail to meet expectations. Raw numbers from standardized tests might also be illustrative. It does make a difference if students are learning what they are supposed to learn, or if they're not.

It also makes a difference if teachers are trying to improve their practice during the progress of their careers. Even good teachers know there are specific things they need to do better in the classroom, yet don't push themselves to improve; and too many teachers have some glaring weaknesses that have long escaped attention. Just as we want to measure student growth in numbers, so we want to measure the growth of teachers. Missouri's system for calculating yearly improvement (or lack thereof) and the 1–7 summative scale ranging over a variety of teaching areas helps teachers and administrators know where teachers stand professionally—both in terms of their own professional growth and in comparison with peers.

If devising better teacher evaluation systems was the singular interest of educational reformers—that is, if reformers were focused only on finding evaluation tools that help teachers identify their weaknesses and deficiencies so they can better help students—then everyone should celebrate the new systems, especially teachers. If this were truly the case, maybe we could even overlook the host of problems that come with reducing complicated practices, such as teaching and learning, to numbers. But despite the rhetoric of reformers and the best efforts of people working in state education departments, we know these new teacher evaluation systems have been devised not simply to support the growth of teachers. They have come about for much less noble or helpful reasons. Teacher evaluation systems intent on value-added scoring procedures and other ways of numerically cataloging teachers arise in concert with, or in the context of, other reform ideas and implemented policies—policies like the repeal (or overhaul) of tenure laws, the repeal of first hired/last fired policies, and the diminishment of union protection, among others. The goal of these policies, taken together, is to be able to fire teachers easily and quickly. The new evaluation systems provide an "objective" way to do this—these assessments providing judgments about teachers that look as if they are documented, reliable, and valid.

Another way to put it is that these new teacher evaluation methods— just like the devising of standards and all the other policies in the reform agenda—send teachers the either/or message discussed above: Either improve your performance, or look for another job. It is a message sent with doubt, mistrust, blame, and resentment aimed toward teachers, and teachers understand this clearly.

Addition and Value: The Governing Metaphors for Teaching and Learning

When standards and curricular objectives become markers of accomplishment; when in every class or grade we make sure we count what students know and can do at the end of a school year and compare it to what they could do at the beginning; when we decide that one teacher is more effective than another based on value-added measurements or some other way of counting accomplishments—then "addition" and "value" become the governing metaphors for teaching and learning. That is, the ideas of addition and value tell us everything we need to know about purposes of education and the tasks of teachers. The purpose of learning is to "get more" and the task of teaching is to "give more," where both the "more" that is gotten and the "value" it has is clearly discernable.

Under the governance of these metaphors, we start to see teaching and learning as a simple addition problem, the kind we've been doing since second or third grade. What the teacher is supposed to do is "add to" what students already know, understand, or can do. The more that gets added in a given year—or the greater the sum at the end of the year—the better. When we see learning primarily as a process of addition, we see it as mounting incrementally—it is the gradual accretion of information and knowledge over time. Learning objectives are expressions of the different knowledge, information, or skill to be added, stated in measurable terms. In this thinking, all information and knowledge is valuable in and of itself. That is, it is good to accumulate a stockpile of things you know, things you can identify, and things you can do, and the object is to make that pile as big as possible. We also hope, of course, that accumulated information and knowledge leads to some set of understandings about certain things we can also identify in curriculum objectives—how government works, for example, or how science and scientists work. Every addition to what a student knows or understands has value—it's important, it makes the student in some sense better. The student is better prepared for future study, for work, to be a better citizen, to realize something better for him or herself. Under the governance of these two metaphors, we see schools as places that literally "add value" to students' lives. And as this happens, of course, schools add value to our society.

Given this thinking, which, of course, reflects something true about teaching and learning, it makes sense for us to test to see how much value a teacher has added to a student's life—whether it's more or less than we expected, more or less than that produced by other teachers. The "addends" we're looking for must be recognizable and describable—they must be discrete, measureable, quantifiable—otherwise we won't know how they add up, and we won't know how to make judgments about teachers. Standards, in the form of curricular objectives, are these addends—the things we look for and measure on standardized tests—and it makes sense that these objectives should "drive" instruction. Administrators or other "managers" of teachers should keep a careful watch on teachers, and they should insist teachers prove that their students are mastering designated objectives. Tight managerial oversight, including weekly meetings with teachers, is warranted "in the spirit of ensuring that every teacher is leading students to fulfill their potential." Anything less would be inexcusable. Teachers who do not add enough value for students ought to be fired.

These metaphors suggest a powerful and attractive pay-off at the end of the day when that sum of learning has gotten large enough. The simplest, clearest, and least objectionable way to describe the ultimate value of ac-

ed learning is to speak of the opportunities learning brings. Learn-
kes things possible. People who have learned valuable and useful
have all kinds of doors opened to them that otherwise would be shut.
We mentioned at the close of Chapter 1 that these educational reforms
are closely tied to a set of widely shared American values, and equal opportunity is certainly one of them. We know that opportunities we have as
individuals are often tied to having a good opportunity to learn in schools.
Our educational history is checkered with various failures to provide equal
schools and equal opportunities to learn, and we know that in many ways,
and in many places, that ideal is still not being met. Educational reformers
expect standards and accountability measures and other reforms—especially choice mechanisms, like charter schools—will put pressure on educators
to address and fix these inequities, especially in urban areas. And implied in
all of this is the same mathematical metaphor we've been talking about: the
greater the learning, the greater the opportunities. More doors get opened
the more you learn.

Knowledge is Power: KIPP Schools and the Promise Made to Students

This payoff of learning is represented in a slightly different way in the
name of the most notable and often cited charter school system in the United States—the KIPP schools. As I noted earlier, KIPP stands for "Knowledge
is Power Program." For those involved in this system, "Knowledge is Power"
is not just a program name—it's an emblem, a mission statement, a statement of faith or commitment—something that orients their every effort.
The famous and powerful phrase "Knowledge is power" dates back at least
to the time of Sir Francis Bacon, the great Enlightenment figure who was
an intellectual reformer, philosopher, and champion of modern science.
Bacon claimed "all knowledge as his province" and dedicated himself to a
wholesale revaluation and restructuring of traditional learning. Knowledge
is power, according to Bacon, not when it is bound to literary and philosophical achievements of the past, but when it is embodied in the form of
new technical inventions and mechanical discoveries that drive history.[10]

The phrase "knowledge is power" begs the question "power to do
what?" Bacon had an answer to that—to have the empirical clarity so that
science and industry can improve the world. The answer for KIPP founders and teachers seems, instead, to bend back to the idea of equal opportunity and equal opportunity to learn, but it does so with a little more
kick to it. At KIPP, learning brings something more than opportunity—it
brings power. We may speak of both opportunity and power as being, in

some sense, "deserved" through the process of learning, but power implies a heightened sense of entitlement and, certainly, a heightened sense of benefit or reward for learning. Opportunity is just a chance at something; power is the possession of something capable of being wielded. Knowledge is the power to have more. Knowledge is the power to possess and command whatever it is you desire. And, of course, implied in all this is that having more power is better than having less power. We have only to scratch the surface in our thinking about this phrase before we encounter the same metaphors of addition and value. If knowledge is the power to have more of what we desire, then more knowledge brings even more power, and greater goods. This is the addition metaphor at work bringing all sorts of fruits to the labor of learning.

The logic and attraction of the phrase "knowledge is power" does not encourage us to question the basic assumption that underlies it and that must, therefore, underlie the name and intentions of KIPP schools—that the "good" of knowledge is in the power it brings its possessor. The moral edge to the idea of power goes unexamined, and so, too, does the possibility that knowledge would be good for something other than power to the one who possesses it—or that knowledge would be good, in and of itself. Certainly KIPP founders and teachers do not question it. Teachers in KIPP schools are, instead, to embrace and think the best about the kinds of "power" knowledge brings. The KIPP website announces that teachers, leaders, and staff at KIPP schools "are united around a shared end goal: to prepare KIPP students to succeed in college and lead choice filled lives."[11] No one could object to that goal—to students having *that* kind of power—especially underprivileged urban students who have often had college and choice filled lives denied to them.

The goal of preparing students "to succeed in college and lead choice filled lives" closes the loop on what is taken by reformers and many others to be a whole and consistent vision of teaching and learning, and it perfectly frames the emotional reasons for educational reform. First of all, in this thinking there is no getting to college and having the power to make rewarding career choices unless teaching is direct, purposeful, and focused on results. Excellent teaching, according to KIPP, "means planning and executing rigorous, engaging lessons that fit into a logical scope and sequence, as well as using student data to assess mastery of objectives and movement toward big goals for student achievement and growth."[12] Daily lessons are to have objectives or aims that are "achievable, rigorous, and measureable."[13] All public schools need to do what KIPP schools do: "relentlessly focus on high student performance on standardized tests and other objective measures."[14] Standards declare what is acceptable and what is insufficient—standards that can be used to measure each and every student, and each and every teacher. The metaphors of addition and value seep through just about every description of this vision of teaching and learning.

Alongside this vision is a set of personal characteristics required of teachers. KIPP teachers are required to embrace a very simple concept: that they "will do whatever it takes to help each and every student develop the character and academic skills necessary for them to lead self-sufficient, successful and happy lives."[15] They are, furthermore, expected to embrace seven character traits necessary for success: zest, grit, self-control, optimism, gratitude, social intelligence, and curiosity. Public school teachers everywhere should have been making this same commitment.

Blame and Resentment Unbound

Reformers, educators, and everyone else can have decent, reasonable conversations about standards, teacher evaluation, and giving students the opportunities they deserve. Or, they can have conversations about standards, evaluation, and opportunities that are heedless of how such things can narrow teaching and learning in really awful ways. Or, they can have conversations about these things that are both heedless of the narrowing and full of blame and resentment aimed at teachers. This last option is the one most people not directly involved with schools and teachers regularly choose.

Standards, teacher evaluation, and opportunities for students make the perfect frame for the resentment of teachers. According to reformers and many others, teachers haven't had the character and commitment to do "whatever it takes" to make sure each and every one of their students acquires the knowledge, skills, and abilities necessary to go to college and lead choice filled lives. They've been too lazy and too interested in themselves to push so hard for each and every student. Neither have they been diligent enough in the planning and execution of their lessons. They have not thought it necessary to "relentlessly" focus on preparing students to achieve clear, distinct, and measurable objectives in ways that clearly show they have added value to students' lives. Lacking skill, intellectual rigor, and character—and consumed by their own interests and protected by tenure, unions, and seniority policies—teachers have failed students. Not only have they robbed them of opportunity, they have robbed them of power that was rightfully theirs. And that is unacceptable. That deserves our moral indignation and disapprobation, and it demands our immediate action. Immediate action, fueled by blame and resentment, means educational reform—big reform, executed now.

Our "fixes" to the problems of the public schools reveal our blame and resentment of teachers. What teachers need, we think, is to have some pressure put on them. Teachers need to work harder and exhibit a clear and unmistakable commitment to students. We demand teachers do "whatever it takes" to help each and every student succeed. To make sure teachers know we mean business, we take away the courtesies and working conditions teachers have enjoyed. We no longer believe they deserve them. We start charter schools and argue for school vouchers to make them compete for students—because competition makes people work harder. We celebrate the success of some charter schools, ignore the failure of others, and argue that everyone should have the choice to send their children to schools where teachers deliver knowledge that leads to college, and to choice filled lives, and to power.[16]

We give teachers and school administrators clear standards—clear markers of the expectations we have for them—then hold them rigidly accountable for meeting those standards. Instead of trusting that teachers are doing what they are supposed to be doing in the classroom, we start to "manage" them. We measure their productivity fastidiously—and we tie teacher effectiveness directly to value-added measures and student scores on standardized tests. We take away their job security and have them labor under a constant fear they will lose their jobs if they do not perform well enough. We threaten to close the lowest performing schools. We don't care if teachers have to work longer and harder to achieve the standards we have imposed on them—if they have to work longer days, weeks, school years. The job simply needs to get done.

We don't worry about teacher turnover. We favor exciting young people with time and energy to put into their teaching—not veteran teachers who have become cynical and dull. We decide to favor people we think are bright and interesting over people who have gone through tired traditional teacher education programs. We want people with grit and determination, willing to bank on their success in a merit-based system. We have ways of making this all sound exciting—like a brand new profession is being created that will attract the best and brightest of our young people—and sometimes we even mean it. The best part of all this is that we can say these things, and mandate these things, without having to admit they come from blame and resentment aimed at teachers—unless we want to. We can turn to reasonable talk about standards, evaluations, and other matters whenever it's more convenient.

If all this doesn't lead teachers to an excited approval and acceptance of the kind Secretary Duncan envisions—if it doesn't always lead to energized teachers, innovative approaches and mission-based schools—at least it leads to diligence, dutifulness, and compliance. And if the conversation about teaching and learning is always and only about how to help students collect knowledge and skills that enable them to live reasonable lives and have some economic power, at least it is a conversation about a goal we can all appreciate. And if the conversation about teaching and learning never turns to consider outstanding teaching—if it is never about what teachers need to think about if they want to become great teachers—at least it's a conversation about what teachers must do in order to be competent. And if all these changes and reforms do not return teachers to the full and heartfelt esteem, affection, and goodwill we believe we deserve, at least teachers will know they need to do the job they have been paid to do. And that is enough.

We don't need teachers to flash happy, loving, and appreciative smiles at their managers when they walk into and out of the school building every day. Solid effort and solid results are what we need. Like the parent with the misbehaving teenager, we just need to make sure teachers do what they're supposed to do.

We just need to make sure everybody gets home by midnight—or else.

Notes

1. Collins, *Good to Great*, 1.
2. Kopp, *A chance to make history*, 64–69.
3. Ibid., 67.
4. Ibid., 68.
5. David Tyack, *The One Best System: A History of American Urban Education* (Boston, MA: Harvard University Press, 1974).
6. Ravitch, 159.
7. "TEAMTN," accessed October 25, 2014, http://team-tn.org/.
8. "An Overview of IMPACT," accessed October 25, 2014, http://dcps.dc.gov/DCPS/In+the+Classroom/Ensuring+Teacher+Success/IMPACT+(Performance+Assessment)/An+Overview+of+IMPACT. Because teacher performance data isn't always the same or isn't always available, teacher evaluation systems (and value-added systems in particular) need to be a little flexible. The band teacher, for instance, can't be evaluated the same way as the English teacher because the same kind of data is not available; neither can the high school math teacher be evaluated in exactly the same way as a second grade teacher. "Group one" teachers in Washington D.C., discussed here, are subject-matter teachers in core areas where standardized test data is generally available.
9. "Teacher Evaluation," accessed October 25, 2014, http://dese.mo.gov/sites/default/files/01-TeacherEvaluationProtocol.pdf.
10. "Francis Bacon, 1561–1626)," *Internet Encyclopedia of Philosophy*, accessed October 25, 2014, http://www.iep.utm.edu/bacon/.

11. "How We Do It," (2014b), accessed October 25, 2014, http://kipp.org/our-approach.

12. "Excellent Teaching," (2014a), accessed October 25, 2014, http://www.kipp.org/our-approach/excellent-teaching.

13. "KIPP Framework for Excellent Teaching," (2014d), accessed October 25, 2014, http://www.kipp.org/files/dmfile/07022012KFET.pdf.

14. "How We Do It—Five Pillars," (2014c), accessed October 25, 2014, http://www.kipp.org/our-approach/five-pillars.

15. "Where Will You Take Us?" (2014e), accessed October 25, 2014, http://www.kipp.org/careers/applicant-faqs.

16. The most comprehensive review of charter school performance is done by the Center for Research on Education Outcomes, at Stanford University. See "National Charter School Study 2013 (PDF)," accessed January 15, 2015, http://credo.stanford.edu/documents/NCSS%202013%20Final%20Draft.pdf.

6

Teachers: Guilty, as Charged

If teachers, as a whole, haven't been found guilty of anything in a court of law, they are facing a variety of charges in the court of public opinion. If we lumped the key claims against teachers together in a legal-sounding summary charge, we might say that teachers are charged with malfeasance of duty. We have heard the claims made against teachers from the outset of the book, and three particular claims surfaced again in our examination of standards and accountability practices in the last chapter. Teachers are charged with not working hard enough, then with being largely ineffective. And they face the moral charge of denying students power—the power to seize what is rightfully theirs in an American society that seems to promise so much.

The individual charged with a crime in our legal system has his or her actions measured against the specifics of a law, most dramatically in a court trial where fairness and explicitness are always to be maintained. Teachers, however, have their behaviors measured against a set of public, but largely unspecified and unexamined assumptions—in this case about the kind and level of effort expected of teachers, about what we mean by effective

Blame Teachers, pages 77–103

teaching, and about the purposes of schools. But it hardly seems fair, or wise, to base widespread reforms of teaching and the public schools on assumptions that go largely unexamined or unchallenged. Some progress in examining assumptions in these three matters is made in what follows.

Doing "Whatever it Takes"

How hard should teachers work?

The question looks a little stark, sitting there all alone. On the one hand, it's a fair enough question all by itself—one that deserves an answer. At the same time, however, it looks like the kind of question that might require us to consider a host of other issues before we can answer it. Hard work must have something to do with the kind of effort teachers make as part of their teaching task. But what do we mean by "effort," and how do we describe or measure that effort? Is effort measured by results, by the presence or absence of certain expected behaviors, by time put in? Who gets to determine what effort is, what effort is adequate, and how that effort is to be marked or noted? And, though we might not want to admit it, we may wonder about the relationship between effort and pay. We noted in Chapter 3 that Arne Duncan wants to pay starting teachers $60,000 a year with salaries topping out at $150,000 a year. If we pay teachers that kind of money instead of what we pay them now, will we expect teachers to work harder? Or, do we think they should work that hard even if we don't pay them that much money?

These are just some of the questions suggested by our somewhat glaring question—How hard should teachers work? It turns out that it might be a lot easier to accuse teachers of not working hard enough than it is to answer the question of how hard teachers should work.

But we have an answer to our question already on the table, so to speak, from our observations about KIPP schools in the previous chapter. We noted in Chapter 5 that KIPP teachers are required to embrace a very simple concept: that they "will do whatever it takes to help each and every student develop the character and academic skills necessary for them to lead self-sufficient, successful and happy lives." Here, there is no other marker for how much effort teachers should expend. Teachers aren't done until each and every student has the necessary character and skills for success. They are to work together as a school community or singly within their own classrooms until this goal is achieved. The question of effort is answered in the phrase "whatever it takes."

On the face of it, "whatever it takes" sounds like the only acceptable answer to the question of how hard teachers should work or how much effort they should supply in their daily tasks. When one's effort is seen as determining whether or not another human being gets to live a happy, successful and self-sufficient life, then nothing less than "whatever it takes" seems acceptable. That's the same kind of standard we erect for people with other lifesaving or life sustaining tasks—policemen, firefighters, or other first responders, for instance, and doctors and nurses working in critical care units. The phrase "whatever it takes" shines a particular light on the personal virtues of people given such critical tasks. It shows a necessary moral commitment and willing self-sacrifice, and it shows the strength, courage, perseverance, and care necessary to make life, and quality life, possible for others. The perfect ideal of this may be the fearless soldier ready to do "whatever it takes" on the battlefield in defense of his or her country—the soldier who is willing to die for the country he or she serves. Or, the ideal may be the dedicated man or woman who gives up every material possession and every earthly comfort to go to deprived or war-torn parts of the world to bring aid and comfort to those who suffer.

The "whatever it takes" phrase is familiar to people in business and the crafts, too. The businessman and the craftsman do whatever it takes to satisfy the customer or do the job right. This commitment is not without a moral side to it, too. The good, fair, and reputable businessman or craftsman does whatever is proper to be done, and whatever needs to be done, to make things right or fair with the customer. But this is not unalloyed virtue. The businessman and craftsman attend to these virtues with their own self-interests at least partly in mind: they tend to the customer because their own job, income, reputation, and future depend on it. But then the same may be claimed about the policeman, firefighter, and teacher who also have self-interests to protect.

We should also note the different pictures we have in mind when we talk about doing "whatever it takes." On the one hand, "whatever it takes" implies the willingness to give up something, or to risk something, that in other circumstances an individual might rightfully choose to preserve, conserve, or protect. The firefighter, policeman, and soldier, for instance, are asked to put their lives on the line. So is the surgeon and the nurse on the battlefield. On the other hand, the doctor and nurse working in a local hospital or surgery center do not incur this same kind of risk. Their lives are not usually in danger, though we can imagine (with the assistance of so many hospital dramas on television) some horrible crisis situation where medical personnel would face similar threats. But typically, in this setting, doing "whatever it takes" means bringing all resources to bear on a problem, and it means doctors and nurses acting with the best possible knowledge, judgment, commitment, and skill as they try to save a life, respond to an injury, or cure an illness. This picture, too, has elements of heroic self-sacrifice in it—part of what we see in the phrase "whatever it takes."

But the phrase also has a more pedestrian sense to it. It points to whatever needs to be done, even if what needs to be done is unpleasant, unwanted, distasteful or is thought unjustified or unnecessary. The businessman may grit his teeth when he mutters the phrase "the customer is always right," and he does not always act with love, compassion and fellow-feeling when he does what the customer asks of him—but he does it, or he risks losing the customer and his reputation. "Whatever it takes" is sometimes less a heroic virtue than an unpleasant necessity, sometimes an economic necessity.

Failure is Not an Option

We can, in each of these instances, link the "whatever it takes" phrase to another one of our favorite phrases: "Failure is not an option." That's the mindset we want and expect from policemen and firemen engaged in a perilous event, from the soldier given a mission on the battlefield, from the businessman out to rescue a client gravitating toward competitors, and from the doctor and nurse involved in a life-saving surgery. And that's the mindset we want from the teacher in the classroom. In KIPP schools, teachers are to make sure—they are to do whatever it takes to make sure—that each and every student develops "the character and academic skills necessary for them to lead self-sufficient, successful and happy lives." Other schools might declare the goal in a slightly different way. But teachers are supposed to ensure that students get what they are supposed to get, or learn what they are supposed to learn. Failure is not an option.

When failure is not an option, a pretty high bar is set for teachers. But the same bar is set for the soldier, the doctor, the nurse, the firefighter, the policeman, and the businessman, and it doesn't make sense to set a bar any lower than this. To do so would be to accept defeat before effort is made. A lower bar might attenuate the kind of commitment, dedication, and enthusiasm necessary for anyone to do their tasks successfully—certainly for teachers to reach each student successfully.

But while we never believe it is a good thing to anticipate failure before we begin an important endeavor (that's a kind of self-defeating behavior that doesn't do us much good) it is, nonetheless, naïve to believe that failure is never an option. Failure is always a possibility—not just for the teacher, but for the soldier, the doctor, the businessman, or the policeman—no matter the skill, commitment, or dedication of those involved or the amount or quality of resources dedicated to achieving a successful outcome. Businessmen lose clients and customers, doctors lose patients in surgery, fire takes away possessions and human life, and teachers fail to reach students. Failure is even more a possibility if one doesn't have adequate resources, or if others do not offer available resources, needed to solve a given problem. The soldier can dedicate him or herself to do "whatever it takes" to win the battle and believe that "failure is not an option." But if that soldier goes into battle without the tools necessary to win it, failure is very much a possibility no matter how heroically the soldier might act. It's the same with teachers.

Of course, it may be that this admission is symptomatic of the failed thinking of the past that Wendy Kopp finds so disappointing. We recall from Chapter 4 what Kopp told her eight year-old son when he asked why Kopp would ask people with no experience, fresh out of college, to solve big problems in education. She acknowledged that experience can be invaluable, but then argued

> ... there's also a power in inexperience—that it can make a huge difference to channel the energy of young people, before they know what's "impossible" and when they still have endless energy, against a problem that many have long since given up on. They can set and meet goals that seem impossible to others who know more about how the world works.

Kopp favors the unremitting optimism and boundless energy of youth. When uttered by a young college graduate and Teach for America cadet, the phrase "whatever it takes" is a mixture of this optimism and energy. It is Kopp's faith, and the faith of David Levin and the people of KIPP schools, that the optimism and energy of the young teacher is powerful enough to surmount the most difficult circumstances deprived or underserved students face in our schools. Positive psychology, or learned optimism, is key not only for teachers, but for students and their parents as well, and it is an essential part of the ideology of KIPP schools.

Setting the Ideal for How Hard Teachers Should Work

We have, then, one answer for how hard teachers should work. It is something of an ideal signaled by a "whatever it takes" approach, and it is epitomized by the optimism and unending energy of young teachers. Just as the soldier (usually thought of as a young man or woman) sacrifices everything to win the battle, the teacher must sacrifice everything to help students succeed. Teachers don't need to be willing to sacrifice their lives for students like soldiers do for their country. But they must be willing to sacrifice other things, especially time, but also physical and emotional energy. And the sacrifice is expected to be considerable. There is only one measure for when a teacher has given enough time and energy—when each and every student has the necessary character and skills for success. Success is the only acceptable measure of effort, and "grit" is as important as heroic idealism in seeing things through to completion.

Observers of KIPP schools report that teachers in charter schools—most of them young—often spend between 60 and 90 hours per week engaged in teaching related tasks.[1] Many teachers in both charter and regular public schools are, after the regular school day, expected to supervise extracurricular activities, offer elective classes, or help students in a tutoring situation. Teachers are being called upon to be available to students and parents for telephone calls or on-line conversations during evening hours and on weekends. Increasingly, parents, school officials, charter school operators and others expect teachers to agree to measures that extend the time teachers spend with students—to increase the length of the school day, extend the school year by two or three weeks, adopt a year-round schedule, or spend time on Saturdays to help struggling students—and to not always demand compensation for this extra time.

Young teachers—many of whom have not yet married or started families—are often better positioned to do "whatever it takes" than many older teachers. Older teachers, or teachers with families or other obligations, have to balance their teaching tasks with these other responsibilities. Younger people usually have more time to give, and their energies and commitments are not so divided. And so they become the more desirable people to hire.

And it is not just the time availability of young people that causes school leaders, especially leaders of charter schools, to hire young people—and it's also not just their self-confidence and unflagging idealism. It is also their readiness to accept diminished working conditions, to accept the elimination of courtesies teachers have always enjoyed. Many young people wanting to become teachers are happy with the changes this round of educational reform is bringing—that tenure is being eliminated, union protectionism diminished, and "first hired/last fired" policies eradicated. And they are typically not so worried about changes to pension plans or the institution of merit pay. Most of these changes mean more jobs will be opening up for them.

The Soldier or the Doctor: Which Ideal for Teachers?

If the teacher is like the soldier, then we know how hard teachers should work and what attitude toward that work they should employ. Teachers should be like the young people Kopp admires—the ones who see these struggling students and will do whatever it takes to help them attain the advantages they deserve. Like the soldier, the teacher is always available, always ready to serve, always willing to sacrifice.

But the "whatever it takes" ideal shifts a bit if we compare the teacher not to the soldier fighting a battle, but to the hospital doctor or nurse fighting to save an ill or injured patient. The ideal remains, but the risks and sacrifices are different. There is no risking of life and limb, but there is still the sacrifice of one's dedication and commitment. "Whatever it takes" means the teacher must bring all possible personal and professional resources to bear on their work with students. Like doctors with their patients, teachers must act with the best possible knowledge, judgment, commitment, and skill in their teaching. They must possess and employ the same kind of personal virtues—moral commitment, self-sacrifice, strength, courage, perseverance, and humanity.

But as we shift away from the soldier and toward the doctor or nurse as the model of "whatever it takes" thinking, several things shift with it. One thing that changes is that the young person characterized by unremitting optimism and unending time and energy is no longer the ideal we have in mind. It isn't how we see the best doctors and the best nurses, and it isn't how we see the best teachers. In place of this image is a person, at least a little older, who has the training and experience necessary to make careful, thoughtful, and wise judgments. One's optimism is not gone—the optimism of youth, we might say—but one is also not heedless of dangers, difficulties, and the possibility of failure. Time and energy are not gone either, but both are more carefully husbanded. In this image, teachers have the same responsibility as doctors—to do what is necessary for students (or patients) to thrive—but like the doctor, the teacher is not solely responsible for failure. Something unforeseen could happen to a patient or student, or a patient or student could refuse the help offered them. And no one asks the doctor or nurse to put everything else in their lives aside in the service of their patients. No one asks them to spend 70 to 90 hours a week with no increase in pay.

But the personal virtues we mentioned—the moral commitment, strength, courage, perseverance, and care—these are not always easy to see, and they are certainly not possible to measure. We tend to trust what we can clearly see when trying to determine the time, effort, care and dedication of teachers. We see effort when we can count the hours teachers spend working. We recognize effort when we see teachers spending time with students after school and when we see the glow of lights from a teacher's classroom as she works into the night grading papers and preparing the next day's lesson. We measure time and effort in the days added on to the end of the year and the number of evening telephone calls teachers make to the parents of struggling students.

And we tend to count a lack of effort in the same visible ways. We become convinced teachers are not working hard enough when we notice that it's teachers who are the first ones out of the building at the end of the school day. And we don't trust they have a "whatever it takes" attitude when they protest the lengthening of the school day, new teacher evaluation measures, or merit pay. We don't trust their virtues when we hear them grousing about their pay instead of articulating their faith in and hope for students. We want to measure their virtue and their effort by what the eyes see and the ears hear, and little else.

But it is hard to see wisdom and judgment at work—and to know what these judgments suggest about the time and effort teachers have put into their work. Moral commitment, dedication, self-sacrifice, strength, courage, perseverance, and care are not always measured by hours spent working with students or recognized in familiar images. As often as not these things reveal themselves "backstage," as it were, or out of the sight of everyone but teachers themselves. Teachers often reveal their commitment and dedication entirely in private—in their inner lives that they share with few people, if they share it at all.

It is next to impossible to describe all that teachers think and worry about, both inside and outside the classroom, when they think about their teaching. In the moment of teaching, teachers think about a multitude of things simultaneously. They think about what is, or is not, going well in a particular lesson, right at the moment it is being taught. What needs to be attended to immediately—what student misbehavior, what look of student disinterest, what explosion of enthusiasm? At any single moment there is a noticing and summing up of what is happening in the classroom even as the teacher's mind jumps ahead and plans what to do next. Then, at the end of the day, come all the reflections: Why didn't this lesson go so well? Why didn't students find this or that compelling? What should I have done when this event happened, or that question, or this problem? What can I do so that my students understand this material? What do I do tomorrow as I pick things up from where I left them today?

The asking and answering of these questions must count as effort or hard work on the part of teachers, even if we can't see it. So, too, must every effort teachers make when they move beyond their immediate reflections about their teaching. We usually don't see teachers when they go looking for new ideas—when they deepen subject matter understanding or think about how to better present material to students. We know teachers talk to one another about these things, but they do many other things as well. They read professional articles and books, and they see things on television or on the internet and think about how ideas there might fit into their teaching. They take classes, acquire advanced degrees, and seek out mentors for advice. They spend summer vacations making new lesson plans or entirely rethinking what they want to do with their classes next year. Teaching is a prism through which they take in the events of the world—always thinking about what they could do with this idea, or that idea, or this event, or that issue.

When we realize that teachers really do such thinking, talking, reading, planning, and study—both formally and informally, both "off the clock" and on the clock—then the notion of "effort" and "working hard" gets complicated. All this thinking and planning must count as time and effort on the part of teachers—just as it does for doctors, nurses, and people in many other jobs or professions. All this must count as "working hard" even though most people will never see any of this going on—even though these things are rarely measured with either the clock or the eye. And the absence of this kind of effort or hard work on the part of some teachers should be as worrisome as a perceived laziness in the classroom.

Teaching is still a time-intensive profession, and clock hours do still matter. But to measure and admire effort simply by counting clock hours, or to hire the optimistic young teacher simply because he or she will volunteer extra hours at school (or because he or she can be easily intimidated into doing so) is naïve, unrealistic, unfair, and, frankly, unadvisable. Neither is it fair to infer effectiveness from the amount of time spent. The inordinate time the young teacher spends is no automatic improvement over the wise decision-making of the veteran teacher. The moment of clarity, elucidation, or enlightenment the wise and gifted teacher can provide for students may be worth more than all the hours spent by the tireless young teacher.

Just a Rallying Cry

"Whatever it takes" is certainly the kind of rallying cry we want teachers to issue, as I suggested above. The phrase expresses the commitment of teachers to make sure students get what they need to live successful and happy lives. But the phrase cannot stand for open-ended expectations for how hard teachers should work, and it should not be issued or understood as an explicit and unyielding demand for perfection on the part of teachers. The measure of the phrase is not the exhaustion of teachers, and neither is it their frustration or their guilt when failure does, indeed, happen. The phrase cannot supply the rationale for dismissing veteran teachers—those "first hired"—who may not stay at school until 7:00 at night, but who have the wisdom and judgment to teach well and who supply continuing effort in different ways. The phrase reminds teachers of the obligations they owe students and the time they must put in, but it cannot mean we believe corps allegiance or naïve optimism is a clear replacement for considered judgment, patience, quiet, or wisdom. And no matter how inspiring the phrase may seem to be, it cannot provide the basis for reasonable, considered, and effective school reform.

The Ineffective Teacher

Teachers face a second charge in the court of public opinion—that too many of them are ineffective. International comparisons seem to suggest this, and so do failed national and state tests, low graduation rates of minority students, and poor academic skills of entering college students. Critics of teachers and the public schools take such things as proof that teachers are ineffective, if not outright incompetent.

Understanding What We Mean by "Effective"

We intend something pretty simple and straightforward when we say that someone, or some thing, has been "effective." A person is effective in doing a task that has been given to him or her when, in doing that task, the desired outcome is achieved. A plumber, for instance, is effective, or has worked effectively, when he successfully unplugs a stopped-up sink, and a computer technician is effective when she takes a frozen-up, virus-infected computer and restores it to working order. A process "works," or is effective, when that process—a manufacturing process, let's say, or some other work related routine—produces the desired results. We may also hope for efficiency and some clear evidence of exceptional skill and aptitude in the doing of such tasks, but the measure of effectiveness lies in the outcome of the endeavor: Is the desired outcome achieved? If the desired outcome is not achieved, then we say the process that was tried or the efforts of the person involved were "ineffective."

This sense for what is effective, or ineffective, is what justifies critics of teachers and the public schools when they declaim the ineffectiveness of teachers and schools. Teachers are not achieving the desired outcome. They are not making sure that every student who graduates from high school has the character and academic skills necessary for them to lead self-sufficient, successful and happy lives. That's failure.

But effectiveness, or success, is only achieved when conditions necessary to that success are realized. Achieving desired outcomes is a sign, first of all, that the people involved have the skills and aptitudes necessary to get the job done correctly, and it is a sign they have the necessary willingness or dedication to do so. They have the stick-to-itiveness or perseverance to battle through any difficulties they may encounter along the way. Achieving desired outcomes also suggests the people involved have the preparation or training required to do the job. It suggests that the work environment has been conducive to success, especially that those trying to achieve the outcome are receiving the proper encouragement and support. The people involved also need to be equipped with the proper tools or equipment—anything from the right wrench, to proper computer software, or to expensive machines. For teachers, it may mean that new textbooks, new computers, suitable student desks, books in the library, or many other things, have been supplied. Of course, it also means that student needs have been taken care of, too—that hungry students have food to eat, that students have adequate supplies, that special student needs are met, etc.

When we assign reasons for a given failure—or when we assign blame—we have, then, several places to look. We may naturally first look at the skills, aptitude, and character of those involved, but we also need to look at preparation, training, work environment, and whether or not those involved were equipped with the proper tools. We also have to look at other factors. Is this failure, this ineffectiveness, a permanent or temporary condition? Are there extenuating circumstances or unforeseen events we must consider? And we always have to determine, as we consider any of these things, what an "excuse" for failure is and what seems like a reasonable and justifiable explanation of why desired outcomes were not realized.

Some tasks are more complicated than others, and they require greater skill, aptitude or training. Some tasks require more, and more sophisticated, tools than other tasks, and some tasks seem more sensitive to conditions in the work environment that have, or have not, been established. It is also the case that effectiveness, understood as the achievement of a desired outcome, is difficult to measure when the desired outcome is complex. It is easier, for instance, to determine if the row of bricks a mason has laid is neat and straight—the desired outcome—than it is to determine if a set of foreign policy initiatives has met the intended objectives. It is also the case that we often need to measure effectiveness with vastly different yardsticks. We prefer quantitative measures whenever possible because numbers make us feel more secure and sure about results we find, but sometimes we need recourse to qualitative or aesthetic measures.

And just a couple more notes about what we mean when we talk of "effectiveness."

Judgment about whether or not some thing, or some person, has been effective is made by means of comparison. We often compare one way of doing things against another, and one person's productive output against another's. In business or healthcare, for instance, we might declare that one way of keeping track of important information about a client, customer, or medical patient is more effective than some other way—that is, one way comes closer to achieving the desired outcome than some other way. Likewise, we can declare one employee to be "better" or more effective than another employee doing the same work because we get more of the desired results. But, at the same time, to declare someone or some thing to be effective is also to judge the quality of a thing, or the performance of people, in relation to its, or their, possible perfection. That is, judgments about effectiveness are made relative to our understanding of what would be a perfect outcome. A person is only effective when he or she achieves or approximates this possible perfection. This standard of perfection has been at the root of our discussion throughout this chapter and is captured in phrases like "whatever it takes" and "failure is not an option." Effective teachers do whatever it takes to make sure *all* their students have the skills and character for success—that is, when perfection is achieved. Or, if we want to be a little fairer to teachers, they are effective when they come near to achieving this perfection.

We noted above that some tasks are more complex than others and that in such cases it may be difficult to determine and measure effectiveness. Different judgments about how straight the mason laid the row of bricks may be entertained, but we are likely to find a wider range of judgments—where those judgments are both rational and defensible—when we try to determine the effectiveness of something more complicated. This suggests that judgments about the effectiveness of someone or something may often be subjective. But, as I also noted above, we try to get past this difficulty by finding ways to measure the effectiveness of some thing or someone by using numbers or statistics. We declare what will count, numerically, as a measure of success of a process or a person's performance, then we go about measuring so we can compare outcomes against one another or against the possible perfection or declared standard. We still might need to consider factors, mentioned above, that can influence production—things like unforeseen events that happen or whether or not employees have been given appropriate tools and proper training and support. But numbers give us confidence that decisions about the effectiveness of someone, or something, are being made based on data—that an objective determination is being made that can show us how well, or how poorly, someone or something has performed.

It is surely the case that we are increasingly able to measure quite complicated phenomena numerically and represent results statistically in such a way that the numbers mean something important—that they are not corrupted by a bunch of things that should have been accounted for, but weren't. And so numbers or statistics put to things as a measure of effectiveness must count for something important. But our urge to get to "the bottom line" numerically or statistically is fraught with danger. That urge shapes how we come to see and understand not just the effectiveness of someone engaged in an endeavor, but the entire endeavor itself. When, for instance, the success of a business is measured only in terms of how much, and how regularly, the "bottom line" increases, and when the effectiveness of employees (especially the sales staff) is determined solely or primarily in terms of that increase, then the purpose of the business and the tasks of employees get significantly narrowed. Numbers determine not just effectiveness, but why the business exists, the kind of place it is, and the kind of people it employs. Numbers can come to determine the ethos of the place.

We may put the worry this way: Before we can judge the effectiveness of someone who works at a complex task—the manager in the business world or the teacher in the classroom—we must properly and fully grasp the complexity of the endeavor in which they are involved. Any measure of effectiveness must comprehend that complexity, not reduce or seek to reshape it. When numbers can reveal something important, they should be used. But when numbers, valid and useful to summarize certain limited aspects of performance, are taken to be decisive about the whole of someone's performance of a far more complex task than those numbers can describe, we have erred. In our attempt to be "objective" and sure in our assessment of success or failure, we fail to ask essential questions: Has our assessment grasped the essence, the heart, of what has been produced or the complex outcome we desire—that which may be beyond numbers? That is, has our confidence in numbers obscured our vision? Is what we take as a "sure sign" of the outcome we desire—in the case of teaching, a sure sign of student learning that we can compute numerically or statistically—really just a partial sign of what we desire, an appearance of what we want, but not the real or whole thing? And does our search for numerical security—our search for partial signs—interfere with, and sometimes make impossible, the deeper, richer and more profound learning that is the outcome we truly desire, or ought truly to desire?

This is not an elaborate argument produced to argue away poor student test scores, and neither is it an effort to protect teachers by keeping the assessment of their performance vague and hazy. But there are at least two reasons why we should be careful how we talk about the *effectiveness* of teachers—teachers taken as a whole, or as individuals. One is, as I have suggested, our penchant for trusting numbers to provide what we want to believe is an objective measure of something, no matter how complex that thing is. And the other is our penchant to reach for the most damning weapons we can find when we want to attack someone or something. When we resent someone or some group of people—as, in this case, we feel betrayed by teachers and aim contempt and malevolence their way—we'll look for anything that makes our argument against them. Numbers that show poor student achievement appear to be just what we need, and so we leap to those numbers and disregard the complexity of the teaching task and obscure any nuanced understanding of what we mean by teaching effectiveness. Our emotions trump our reason. We make the argument we want to make regardless of how unfair it might be and heedless of how our understanding might keep us from truly helping teachers and improving their performance.

In Pursuit of the Effective Teacher and the Effective School

We have not always talked about the *effective* teacher or the *effective* school. In fact, we have only done so for the past 30 years—a significant chunk of time, but relative to how long we've been talking about teachers and schools, a literal drop in the bucket. But what a decisive 30 years it has been.

In 1966, University of Chicago sociologist James Coleman published his landmark study, *Equality of Educational Opportunity* which examined the effects of family on schooling.[2] Coleman argued that schooling accounted for only about 10% of the variance in student achievement. The remainder was accounted for by students' ability/aptitude, socio-economic background, and home environment. And in 1972, Christopher Jencks et al. published *A Reassessment of the Effect of Family and Schooling in America*—a book that expanded Coleman's argument about what little effect schooling had on the future success of graduates.[3] Jencks et al. argued, among other things, that even if we could somehow equalize the reading ability of every student—what we now take to be essential if students are to lead self-sufficient, successful and happy lives—we would still not appreciably reduce the number of people who endure economic hardships in the future. Schools and teachers just don't have that much effect on student achievement or the future success of students. A family's socio-economic level and the education attained by the mother and father decide much more about the achievement and success of students than does anything that happens to students in school.[4]

That's a tough pill to swallow for those who see education as a great social and economic equalizer, and educators all over the country were quick to try to disprove the theses of Coleman and Jencks. But how could these ideas be disproven? The answer to this question started to come in 1982—and with it came the birth of effective schools research and our belief that we could talk meaningfully about effective teaching and effective teachers.

Michigan State sociologist Wilber Brookover and his colleagues embarked on a series of studies in schools serving economically poor students who—despite the predictions of Coleman and Jencks—were succeeding quite nicely in school.[5] Brookover set out to determine what it was in those particular schools, and what was happening in those classrooms, that made this success possible. He concluded that "achievement . . . is highly related to the organization [of the school]" and also that "any child can learn if we provide the appropriate teaching-learning environment."[6] Brookover, and many others, believed they had found a way to silence the pessimistic outlook of Coleman and Jencks. What we needed to do was find out why certain schools, and certain teachers, were having success in teaching even the most hard to reach students. How were these schools organized? What teaching techniques and behaviors were being used? What was effective, and what was ineffective? Once we knew the answers to these questions, we would know how to improve schools and teaching and learning within them. And we would know how to give every student a chance to live a good and productive life—not just students from privileged families.

Brookover and his associates were among the very first to engage in this kind of thinking about schools, and they are credited with creating the *effective schools movement.* That movement has led to mountains of research about schools and teaching—research about better and best ways of organizing schools and conducting teaching—research that continues to multiply. This continuing research about "what works," or what is effective, shapes curricular and instructional decision-making in schools, and it shapes the professional development activities of teachers and the content of teacher education programs. It shapes educational policy-making at local, state, and national levels, and it drives the design of such things as elementary reading programs and high school mathematics textbooks. It also supports the impulse to test students, especially with standardized tests. It is a kind of common sense for educational researchers and practitioners alike that we cannot know what works with a wide variety of students in a variety of different schools unless we test for results.[7]

Having Power Over Teachers

This kind of research about schools and teaching dominates educational decision-making for good reason. This research appeals to a simple logic or manner of thinking about things that we all share. In just about every task we do in life—from cooking a dinner to teaching someone how to read—there is more than one way to get it done. We have to decide how we are going to accomplish the task that is in front of us, and we naturally wonder about which of the different ways of accomplishing our task would give the best results. Would the dish I'm preparing turn out better if I did it this way or that way? Would this child learn to read better, and want to read more, if I taught with a phonics approach or a whole language approach? How can I know? I want to do it the best way—the most effective way. I don't want to make a mistake. Is there any empirical evidence that if I do the task this way, or that way, I'll get better results?

It is certainly not the case that we only started worrying about better and worse ways of doing things in schools and classrooms when Brookover responded to the ideas of Coleman and Jencks. Conversations about better and worse ways of teaching and organizing schools have gone on forever. But empirical researchers, especially since the early eighties, have been able to make claims about school organization and effective teaching methods that relatively few before them were able to make: They are able to say that their ideas are *evidence based* or *data based*. One reading program works better than another, or one way of teaching a mathematical concept works better than another, not based on hearsay or the power of established practice, but on evidence. Research has produced data from which conclusions can be drawn. And while research may be flawed and both the process of the research and the findings drawn from it can be disputed, we have an abiding faith that more and better research will eventually lead us to doing things better or more effectively.

So it makes sense, then, to talk about *effective teaching*—to talk about what works, what is evidence-based, or what the data reveals to us. And it makes sense to learn how to teach, or to change one's teaching, in accord with what the data reveals. What could justify staying with a particular teaching technique or behavior that just doesn't work as well as some other technique or behavior? It appears that only a certain kind of stubbornness or laziness would keep a teacher from a positive change in his or her practice warranted by carefully crafted and thoroughgoing research. And it makes sense to believe that teaching is improved, and schools are improved—and most importantly, that student learning is improved—when this research is brought to teachers and, by some means, they are encouraged or required to change their practice.

This is the thinking that justifies Missouri's new Educator Evaluation System (discussed in Chapter 5) where teachers, in consultation with their principal or other supervisor identify three weaknesses in their teaching that need to be rectified. They find research-based solutions to their problems that will make them more effective in the classroom. And it justifies the management approach of KIPP schools, and traditional public schools, too, that we also discussed earlier (Chapter 5). Remember, Wendy Kopp wants every teacher to have weekly one-on-one meetings with his or her "manager" where the teacher's progress toward various performance goals is assessed. These sessions are to be informed by data about student learning—about what is working, or what is *effective*. If something is not working, the manager is there to suggest or require some change to more effective methods. These regular student assessments and the weekly meetings with managers are conducted, we recall, "in the spirit of ensuring that every teacher is leading students to fulfill their potential" and to ensure that everyone is meeting the standards expected of them.

None of this is as neat and unproblematic as some people want it to be. We may still worry, as we did above, if all such claims about effectiveness capture the nuance and complexity of teaching and learning. We ought to realize, for instance, how we impoverish the idea of an education by conceiving it only or primarily as an aggregation of skills or abilities—as a mere addition problem. We ought to realize how a teacher's other gifts or attributes may get lost or muted when that teacher is forced to adopt certain "best practices" given the stamp of approval by some "manager." We ought to realize that the greatness we should want teachers to realize is so much more than any measure of "effectiveness" gleaned from a pile of data.

But effective schools research can be and is being used as a lever to encourage or force teachers to change their practices—all in the name of what works to improve student achievement in schools, with an accompanying faith that increased achievement portends a brighter, happier, and more economically secure future for students. The clarity of empirical research gets married to an ethical argument about doing what is best for students. This makes it difficult, if not impossible, for teachers to register any kind of counter-argument to the findings of what is taken to be true and indisputable—to mount any kind of knowing resistance to practices buttressed by evidence and data. Resistance looks like an expression of ignorance or baseless selfishness. Or, it looks like just plain orneriness. And it certainly provides a basis for terminating teachers who resist the changes dictated by the research and insisted upon by supervisors.

The Aims and Purposes of Schools

As we noted previously, a clear vision or purpose for schools emerges from arguments about how hard teachers should work and why they need to adopt effective, evidence-based practices that lead to maximum student achievement. This vision is widely shared and has been for a long time. We can put it this way—a kind of mission statement for public schools and teachers:

> Teachers need to work hard and do whatever it takes to make sure students acquire sufficient knowledge and skills as well as workable habits of mind. Teachers need to make sure they are effective, and they need to choose ways to teach that lead to distinct, measurable student achievement. All teachers need to do this so that all students—not just students from privileged backgrounds—have a full set of life options.

This is, as we have seen, just the mission so many people believe schools and teachers do not fulfill. Teachers do not work hard enough because they do not care enough, and this, coupled with sloppy and ineffective teaching, means students do not come out of school with the necessary knowledge, skills, and habits of mind. And that means students—especially underprivileged students—don't have a full set of life options.

The phrase "a full set of life options" sets the primary aim and purpose of schools in today's educational conversation.[8] Set in the context of our perceived failure to provide those options to students in our poorer communities, the phrase, when used by reformers, marks our hope that schools still can—if reformed—help us achieve our highest and most noble desires: that equality will prevail, that schools can provide everyone an equal opportunity to succeed in life. We look around our nation and see a vast disparity in income, power, wealth, and health—and we want to connect that disparity to inequalities in education. If schools can provide that full set of options for each and every student, we will achieve not just the critical goal of equal educational opportunity but some measure of equal educational outcome, as well. And that should lead to greater economic and social equality.

The phrase also speaks to us in quite personal ways. We all want to have a wide range of options—not just educational options, but options of all sorts. We want to have for ourselves the same kind of options everyone else has, including options the most privileged among us seem to enjoy. And the phrase reflects the ways parents have always thought about these things when thinking about their children. Parents speak of wanting something better for their children than what they had when they grew up, and that certainly means having more life options.

The phrase "a full set of life options" is as non-prescriptive as it is egalitarian. Like our cherished American phrase "life, liberty, and the pursuit of happiness," this phrase does not recommend one life option over another. To have options is to have the power to possess what it is we want to possess—as we discovered in our reflection on the phrase "Knowledge is power" in Chapter 5. Certainly, we mean by this not just the opportunity for all students to go to college, but the opportunity for them to have a career and a lifestyle of their own choosing. And we mean for them to have the means to make money and to possess the things they desire. The phrase means being able to have what other people have.

The "gods" of Economic Utility and Consumerism

If the "life options" phrase is not emotionally stirring as an expression of the aim or purpose we have for education, it does have several advantages. First of all, the phrase is largely unobjectionable. No one would suggest that a young person graduating from high school should want or deserve a less than full set of life options. The phrase also directs educators to make sure that education is useful and practical. Teaching and learning is to have a clear and tangible outcome. Students must easily and readily see the value of what they are learning.

Students have always needed a reason to go to, and learn, in schools. Neil Postman, in *The End of Education: Redefining the Value of School*, suggests students need a reason "for being in a classroom, for listening to a teacher, for taking an examination, for doing homework, for putting up with school even if they are not motivated."[9] Students who believe they will acquire a full set of life options if they go to school and do what is asked of them have, it would appear, the best possible reasons for learning. Students will put up with the trappings and requirements of school because there is a promise at the end. Learning adds up, and if students stick with it they will receive a pay-off at the end. That pay-off is that they can get what they want. The pay-off is power. It is especially the power to get a good job so they can command a certain kind of wealth and have what they want to have.

Postman calls this the "god of Economic Utility." It is a "god" (in the small *g* sense of the word) because it gives meaning and purpose to our learning—it is a compelling narrative that shapes our needs and aspirations, and we organize ourselves around it.[10] But, according to Postman, this is not a specially benevolent or kind god:

> As its name suggests, it is a passionless god, cold and severe. But it makes a promise, and not a trivial one. Addressing the young, it offers a covenant of sorts with them: If you will pay attention in school, and do your homework, and score well on tests, and behave yourself, you will be rewarded with a well-paying job when you are done. Its driving idea is that the purpose of schooling is to prepare children for competent entry into the economic life of a community. It follows from this that any school activity not designed to further this end is seen as a frill or an ornament—which is to say, a waste of valuable time.[11]

The god of Economic Utility is automatically coupled with another god, the god of Consumership. This god provides an answer to the question, If I get a good job, then what?[12] The god of Consumership teaches students that the primary reason for learning has to do with economics—with having stuff, hopefully the "good stuff," when they are older. According to Postman, both of these gods urge us to see ourselves as economic creatures and teach us that our sense of worth and purpose is to be found in our capacity to secure material benefits. We're best when all of life's options are open to us—especially the best and most economically rewarding of them.

Most of us will tend to think these gods work just fine with students—or that they can be made to work if teachers, parents, policymakers, and others consistently and fervently tell this gospel to young people as they move through the school system. The narrative is not new with KIPP schools and the arguments of people like Wendy Kopp. Most of us have had this kind of story pounded into us since we were very young. Certainly, students hear the gods of Economic Utility and Consumership preached all the time—from the front of classrooms, at their kitchen tables, in the Oval Office, and everywhere in-between. If there were ever a tool with which a teacher might wrench some effort and study from students, this ought to be it.

One of the reasons we believe this story is that it speaks to something real: at some point, we need to get a job if we want to feed and clothe ourselves, and a job that pays us well is better than one that pays poorly. And to have more and better choices about the jobs we can get is better than being locked into working at a fast food restaurant for the next 40 years. And it's better than being chronically unemployed. And it's certainly better than being imprisoned for something we've done when our lives have gone awry. And we all ought to be able to recognize the better options from these worse ones.

This job story is tied to a moral story we also believe in—the story about the value of hard work. The god of Economic Utility rewards productivity, efficiency, and organization, and it penalizes inefficiency and sloth.[13] These are issues of character as much as requisites for economic success. They are related to the Protestant ethic that has always been dear to our American identity. In this story, hard work and a disciplined capacity to delay gratification are the surest path toward earning God's favor—and a good job.[14] We learned early on from Benjamin Franklin and all manner of other people that good things come to the person who adopts these sturdy and steadfast traits. A part of our American story and identity is, also, distinctly economic. Our sense of worth and purpose is found, at least in part, in our capacity to secure material benefits for ourselves and those we love.[15]

Are These Failed Gods?

To suggest that the gods of Economic Utility and Consumership ultimately fail—that they are as much embarrassingly wrongheaded as they simply fail to give students reasons to learn—seems like more than a misstep. It seems like cultural blasphemy, like a denial of sincere and profound cultural understandings and moral commitments. And it seems to deny the most obvious lever for learning available for use by teachers. Most students come to school dreaming of "what they are going to be when they grow up." Many dream of being rich and famous one day—of living in a big house, of driving a fancy car, and of taking long and expensive vacations to exotic places. If these dreams become more prosaic as children come to realize that certain fantasies are out of reach, still, the "what are you going to do when you grow up?" question persists. And why wouldn't someone's natural desire to want something better for himself—not just something better for himself, but real power and control—be the very heart and soul of his reason for learning? Why would this be wrongheaded, and why wouldn't it work?

But there *are* reasons to reject this god—that is, to reject this story as a reason for learning. And the principal reason is that the story is patently untrue. There simply is no guarantee, anymore, that a good job awaits someone who does reasonably well in high school or college.[16] Those days are gone. Technology has wiped out many good jobs, and not just in industry and manufacturing. It has also wiped out many white-collar jobs—jobs in accounting, architecture, and engineering, for instance. Out-sourcing of jobs to foreign countries has wiped out many more jobs, and so have persistent economic downturns. It is true that the very best of our top college graduates will find employment in jobs that do, indeed, pay well and offer them the consumer and cultural power they desire; and there are jobs in certain sectors of the economy that require a very particular set of vocational skills that can pay well. But the fastest sector of job growth in our economy is in the service industry—jobs in restaurants, retail sales, telemarketing, and the like—and that has been true for a long time now. Most of these jobs are neither well-paying nor personally satisfying. They typically do not yield economic power and a full set of life options.

This doesn't mean, however, that some students don't still trust this story and look to these gods for reasons why they should do well in school. An appeal to an envisioned future works like a charm for many of our best students who are working to get a scholarship or gain admission to their dream college. These students know how to "do school" to get what they want.[17] They are ever mindful of how academic performance and school obligations connect to the future they (or their parents) have envisioned for them, and they do everything they can to make scholarships and college dreams happen. Something similar is true for less driven students who, nonetheless, have always considered themselves to be college-bound. These students tend to school matters well enough to get into college and preserve their plans for the future. It's the students who by instinct, background, or circumstance do not demonstrate this futures-oriented thinking that worry reformers. And they worry teachers, too, though now teachers don't get much credit for this. These students need the constant encouragement of teachers. According to reformers, they need teachers to show them the goods that are theirs in the future if they but attend seriously to their work in school. Teachers must do whatever it takes to get students to work hard for the good future that awaits them. Failure is not an option.

Postman writes of a ten year-old boy he once knew who, upon being asked what he wanted to be when he grew up, answered without hesitation, "An orthodontist"—an idea, Postman concluded, that had to have been put into his head by the child's parents. "It is hard to imagine a more depressing answer," Postman writes.[18] But here Postman is wrong. There are, indeed, more depressing answers. I remember hearing a report some time ago about the job ambitions of young Black students who endured tough circumstances—young people who regularly watched as friends and relatives were led off to jail. These students wanted to be prison guards when they grew up and were ready for their first good job. They knew that it was a lot better to be on the guard side of the prison bars than the prisoner side. Being a prison guard, offered them lots more life options. Lots more power. Lots more freedom.

If teachers can give *all* students a vision of future economic possibilities, even those students coming from the toughest and most disadvantaged of circumstances—and if teachers can inculcate in those students the habits of industry and self-discipline required to realize that future—then, many would argue, teachers will have accomplished the most valuable and difficult task given to them. This justifies the overwhelming presence of these economic gods in schools. It is especially what justifies these gods in charter schools where discipline, order, obedience and learned optimism are stressed or insisted upon.

Devotees of these gods are not worried that this is a crudely utilitarian reason for learning. They do not see it as narrow and unlovely. They find nothing wrong with a ten-year old child saying he wants to be an orthodontist when he grows up. It is nothing over which, like Postman, one should get depressed. On the contrary, it's a good thing. It's certainly a lot better than the alternative—that the child has no reason to learn and, in performing poorly in school, gives himself little or no chance to live a happy and successful life.

Finding Better Reasons for Learning

But others find something lifeless and grim in these reasons for learning—something that suggests we should declare these gods ugly and misbegotten, if not altogether failed. Critics of these reasons are not willing to let these gods make learning in school seem to students like nothing more than an unavoidable passage to what is really valued—being free of school and free of learning in the enjoyment of an easy and prosperous life. They do not want these gods to diminish the idea of learning as they amplify a limited sense for the advantage of learning.

We see something like this worry—and, in addition, intimations about better and deeper reasons for learning—in this short passage from *The Moral Life of Schools* by Philip Jackson, David Hansen, and Robert Boostrom. In one part of the book, they tell the story of "Mr. Peters," a high school religion teacher, who decided to take down a sign hanging in the front of his classroom that said (interestingly enough) "Knowledge is power" in big, black letters. "I remember taking it down," Mr. Peters said:

> . . . because it—I found that it didn't express what I wanted to have in my class. . . . Upon reflection and upon just considering what I'm teaching and considering the symbols I want to convey—that wasn't one of them. And just the way it was up there, in big, black block letters, you know, conveyed power in a certain way. And the dryness of knowledge, you know, just knowledge. For some reason that meant something to me after my first year [in this school]. And I really wanted to convey how important knowledge was and

that you needed knowledge. But after having it up there and going through another year, I felt that raw knowledge isn't what I'm about and neither is power, at least the type of power that seems to be expressed in that [display]. So for my classroom, it became a little too stark.[19]

Now, some may think Mr. Peters worries too much about things his students may not even notice or put together for themselves—here the "Knowledge is power" sign in front of the classroom. But most of us want to believe that the things we say and signal to students actually make a difference to them. Mr. Peters became uncomfortable with the reason for learning implied by the "Knowledge is power" sign. It wasn't the right moral message. He wanted to stand for something else in his teaching; he wanted students to see some other value and reason for learning—perhaps something more nuanced and harder to get at, but something even more meaningful and provocative.

Any teacher who has cared for his or her craft will have had moments like Mr. Peters when doubts arise about his or her teaching, especially the reasons for learning he or she offers students in hopes they will care for what is happening in the classroom. But those better reasons—those reasons that can potentially engage students in their learning in deep and significant ways—seem harder to talk about. And probably harder, still, to give to students in clear and effective ways.

Conclusion

Then, for the third time in this chapter, we have reached the same conclusion: that there seems to be something more in teaching and learning than what we can easily see, evaluate, measure, or even talk about. Something escapes us when we try to count the efforts of teachers and precisely measure their effectiveness, and something gets warped or damaged when our hopes and intentions for students and the reasons we give them to learn get expressed solely or primarily in economic terms. But that doesn't stop us. We like to see things in numbers, in quantities, in data, in totals. We like to count and compare. We think we see things clearly when numbers measure more and less. More hours spent by teachers and higher test scores mean more student learning. More achievement means more life options, more salary, more power, and more material goods. All this makes for a simpler conversation about schools, teaching, and learning—and when the numbers aren't what reformers and policy-makers want to see, they believe they have clear reasons to call for educational reform.

There isn't much sympathy among educational reformers, policy-makers and many citizens for a more nuanced, deeper and richer conversation about teachers, teaching, and the purposes of schools. When educators start talking about how "complicated" teaching and learning is, and about how numbers don't show everything important about what is going on in schools, many see a smokescreen—a bunch of teacher-talk designed to protect teachers from criticism rather than a true and accurate description of the circumstances of teaching. Numbers and evidence are what matter. Results matter and success matters. Everything else is just a rationalization of failure.

I do not know if reformers and others who hold this view—including many teachers, school administrators, and many others in the field of education—can be persuaded to see things differently. There certainly is sense in the concerns they raise. Teachers *do* need to work hard, and they need to worry about being effective in what they do, and they need to prepare students to lead rich and full lives. I hope I have, in what I have written here, acknowledged these things. In no sense do I want to talk my way around them.

But the comfortable, cohesive, commonsense picture of teaching and learning that emerges in this perfect marriage of measureable effort, measureable achievement, and economic gain is simply misleading. It misdirects our efforts to understand teaching and learning, and it misdirects our efforts to improve it. It leaves out too much that is essential to what we must want for our students and teachers in their work together in classrooms. There is more to teaching and learning that not only doesn't get captured in these formulations, but, even worse, gets obscured by them. This is what Mr. Peters sensed as he reflected on the "Knowledge is Power" sign hanging in his classroom. Mr. Peters realized the sign said something important, but it left something out. Mr. Peters couldn't immediately put his finger on what was missing, but he knew something was. That "something" may be very difficult to describe and talk about, but it ought to count for something in any discussion of Mr. Peters' teaching—or anyone's teaching. It ought to count as we think about the effort, the effectiveness, and the value teachers provide their students.

But if Mr. Peters cannot say any more about the reasons he wants to give his students for learning, or the moral messages he wants to send, that does not excuse us from saying more. If the economic gods are to be declared impotent, then others must be suggested and shown how they can give students reasons for being in a classroom, for listening to a teacher, for taking an examination, and for doing homework and all the rest of the work teachers ask them to do. And while we may locate much better and more suitable reasons for learning in the pages of philosophy of education textbooks, we may be afraid that dusty, distant, and formal reasons will fail to resonate with young people, and with their teachers, in our complicated and sometimes gritty world. We need reasons to learn that speak to us—to students and their teachers—reasons that work in real classrooms in sometimes really tough places. It's in the search for these better reasons, and in the attempt to put them to use in the classroom, that we find better and clearer ways to talk about teacher effort and effectiveness.

It is also, incidentally, the much better and legitimate way we can, when necessary, talk about blaming teachers. And it's a much better and more productive way in which to talk about educational reform.

Notes

1. Jim Horn, "A Former KIPP Teacher Shares Her Story," *Schools Matter*, accessed October 25, 2014, http://www.schoolsmatter.info/2012/09/a-former-kipp-teacher-shares-her-story.html.
2. James S. Coleman, et al., *Equality of Educational Opportunity* (Washington, D.C.: U. S. Department of Health, Education and Welfare, 1966, FS 5.238.38001).
3. Christopher Jencks, et al., *Inequality: A Reassessment of the Effect of Family and Schooling in America* (New York, NY: Basic Books, 1972).
4. Philip Cusick, "Why Do Kids Hate School? Why Do We Care?" in *Why Kids Hate School*, ed. Steven P. Jones et al. (Dubuque, Iowa: Kendall/Hunt Publishing Company, 2007) 4, 5.
5. Wilber Brookover, et al., *Creating Effective Schools* (Holmes Beach, FL: Learning Publications, Inc., 1982).
6. Ibid., 78, 2.
7. See "Learning for All," accessed October 25, 2014, http://www.effective-schools.com/. Also see "What Works Clearinghouse," Institute of Education Sciences, accessed October 25, 2014, http://ies.ed.gov/ncee/wwc/.
8. We encountered the phrase "a full set of life options" in Chapter 4. It's from Wendy Kopp's book, *A Chance to Make History* (2011) 9.
9. Neil Postman, *The End of Education: Redefining the Value of School* (New York, NY: Alfred A. Knopf, 1995), 4.
10. Ibid., 5–7.
11. Ibid., 27–28.
12. Ibid., 33.
13. Ibid., 28.
14. Ibid., 14.
15. Ibid., 28.
16. Ibid., 30. See also Jean Anyon, *Marx and Education* (New York, NY: Routledge, 2011).
17. Denise Pope, *Doing School: How We are Creating a Generation of Stressed-out, Materialistic, and Miseducated Students* (New Haven, CT: Yale University Press, 2003).

18. Postman, 30.
19. Philip W. Jackson, Robert E. Boostrom, and David T. Hansen, *The Moral Life of Schools* (San Francisco, CA: Jossey-Bass, 1998), 283.

7

Giving Students Good Reasons to Learn

There's probably not a middle or high school teacher in America who has not heard the following, at least a time or two, from a frustrated or disgruntled student. Forgive the language, but it's the way students tend to speak when they are confused or see no reason to learn what the teacher is teaching: "This sucks," they'll say. "Why do we need to learn this? We're never going to use it." And it's not just middle and high school teachers who hear this complaint. There are no doubt more than a few elementary teachers who have heard it, too.

It's never a great moment for a teacher when this question airs publicly in the classroom. The question can sound like an overt challenge to the teacher's authority or a cruel criticism of his or her teaching ability. It can be a real blow to the teacher's ego. Furthermore, at least from my experience as a high school English teacher, students usually ask this question at exactly the moment when the teacher is least able to answer it—when even the teacher is frustrated with how the lesson is going or when the lesson is less than exciting or distinctly purposeful. These are vulnerable and potentially embarrassing moments for the teacher. That's one reason why teachers don't always give satisfactory or civil responses to this kind of student question. "Because I said so," or "Because it's going to be on the test," or "One more word out of you and. . ."—these are not responses to be proud of.

It took me a while to see these questions from students, no matter when they were uttered or in what tone, as exactly the right questions for them to ask. These are *their* questions and it is natural they ask them. And I realized that these questions deserve a good answer—an answer not from *my perspective*, as a teacher, but from *their perspective*, as students. The teacher might have lots of reasons for teaching something, and teaching it in a particular way. Curriculum standards, printed curriculum, the set-up of a textbook, school or department policies, an upcoming standardized test, or "the way it's always been done"—these are all reasons for teaching something and teaching it in a certain way. But they aren't reasons for students. Students don't care about such things at all. Nor should they. They want, need, and deserve reasons for learning that *they* find compelling.

This does *not* mean that the curriculum must be set up and delivered in accord with the particular and limited tastes, desires, inclinations and preferences of students. I am not suggesting that teachers accede to the desire of many students to get by with doing minimal and minimally acceptable work. Nor am I suggesting that the curriculum must always be made immediately and crudely "relevant" to students' lives—a sort of litmus test students sometimes apply to their studies. But I am suggesting that when students dare to ask the "why" question (either rudely or much more subtly) that teachers have an answer—a genuine, sincere, even provocative answer that can show students why what they are learning is important *to them.* What is even better, of course, is to "beat students to the punch," to borrow a phrase from the world of boxing—to answer students' "why" questions before they even ask them. When the compelling, interesting, and provocative "why" is put at the center of all classroom endeavors, rude interjections disappear almost completely. Or, when they do occur, the teacher is ready for them. Such questions are opportunities for the teacher to remind students of what had been said before—to connect particular learning to the larger task, or to deepen or expand previously given reasons for learning.

Joining Learning Clubs

It may sound a little strange to say it, but when teachers are teaching, they do not, first and foremost, worry about whether or not students are mastering what they are trying to teach them. At least that is not naturally what they think about first when left to their own devices—when someone isn't looking over their shoulder and harping about standards and accountability. The more pressing, telling, and critical worry teachers have *is whether or not students are attending to the lesson being offered in the classroom*. That is, they worry about students being *engaged* in their learning—first, whether or not they are doing what they are supposed to be doing, but, and even more, whether or not they seem *intent* on the task they've been given. Do students seem serious, or earnest, or purposeful as they engage in the learning activities? Has something captured their attention? Do they seem to care about what they are doing?

Teachers assess such things at a glance when they look out at students engaged in doing what they have been asked to do—whether that's working in groups, having a class discussion, or working quietly at their desks. When students plainly care about what they are learning—when they anticipate it, when they work diligently, when they lean forward in their chairs and attend to everything that gets said in a classroom—these are signs of engagement, and they are the first indicators teachers have that the lesson is going to be successful. What they see does not prove that students have learned, or mastered, some particular thing at the center of the lesson, as so many advocates believe standardized tests will prove, but they are surely reliable signs that learning is taking place. Furthermore, they are hopeful signs that learning is likely to continue—that students are "hooked," that they now "get it," and that they want to continue thinking about the subject matter.

In *The Book of Learning and Forgetting*, Frank Smith offers a metaphor for this kind of engagement—the metaphor of a *club*.[1] Most of us, at some point or another in our lives, have been members of some sort of club, either in or out of school—maybe the chess club, or a social club, or even some sort of informal association. Clubs are formed when people share similar interests, and we don't join a club or stay in it if we can't identify with the other club members. As we decide to join a club, we decide we want to be like the other club members, and so we start watching what others are doing, and we try to do what they do.[2] If we can't quite do everything others seem able to do, it's no big deal. Some more experienced club member will show us what to do or help us understand what we need to understand. They don't *teach* us, Smith maintains, so much as they *help* us.[3] Learning is a natural consequence of being in the club—not something strained, forced or artificial.

The teacher who looks out at her students engaged in a learning activity wants to see this kind of club-like behavior. She wants to see students who believe themselves to be members of a club—the reading club (if it's a reading activity or a reading class), or the mathematics club, or the science club, or the history club. The quality of a student's engagement in the activity will tell the teacher if that student believes he or she is a member of the club. If students believe they are *in the club*, then they want to do what more experienced members of the club—especially the teacher—can do, and they want to know what those more experienced members know. And if they *don't* believe themselves to be members of the club—that is, they don't feel they belong and that they are not welcome in the club—then they want nothing to do with club activities. They don't want to read, or work mathematics problems, or learn things about science or history.

Clearly, what matters most is *being in the club*—that is, what matters is encouraging students to join all the different learning clubs so they have a chance to know and do the same things as more experienced members of those clubs. What students actually know and can do when they join a particular club doesn't matter at all. And neither does it matter that at any particular designated time—say, by standardized testing time in the spring—that students know some particular list of things. If students don't know them yet, they will, eventually, as long as they stay as members of the club. They will because they want to know and someone will show them when the time is right.

High-stakes standardized tests, Smith argues, do not encourage students to join these learning clubs.[4] All standardized test scores do for students is identify which of them are already members of a given learning club and which of them are not. And test preparations—the review, the list of things to be known, and the hurried practice to hone certain skills—do not help struggling students want to join a particular club. Such things can look like a "members only" activity. The learning is all strained, forced, and artificial.

When Students are "In the Club"

The club metaphor reminds us of several things essential to teaching and learning. First of all, it reminds us how carefully teachers need to tend to the classroom environment. Teachers need to make sure students feel secure and comfortable while in their classroom. Even more, they must make students feel like they belong there. Teachers need to draw students together and create a community of learners. How long this might take and what it might involve is impossible to say exactly. A kindergarten teacher dealing with students coming to school for the first time would go about this in a very different way than a high school teacher dealing with older students, many of whom now resent having to come to school; and the teacher working with a heterogeneous group of students may have more work to do than a teacher working with a more homogeneous group.

Smith's metaphor reminds us, however, that this sense of belonging is subject-bound or learning-bound. That is, students need to belong not just to a group of congenial people who seem friendly and inviting enough, but to a group of congenial people who do the work involved with club activities—here, that they do what they need to do to learn the subject matter. The teacher extends the initial and continuing invitation to join the club via curriculum and pedagogical choices as much as he or she does by means of an inviting personality. Certainly there are key moments when students decide whether or not they want to be members of a given club—when they are confused or frustrated, for instance, or as they take note of how teachers respond to them verbally in class or infer how teachers view them from teacher comments on written work. These are moments when the dispositions or virtues of the teacher are most important—when she needs to be kind, patient, understanding, or empathetic if the student is going to become or remain a member of her club.

The metaphor also draws attention to teaching and learning when it's at its best or most ideal. There are moments in classrooms, often fleeting, when some aspect of the subject matter captivates teacher and learners— when everyone gives over their entire attention and concern to what is being discussed, explained or understood. At such moments everyone is at least temporarily "in the club," and they are doing the work that is supposed to be done in that particular club. These are intoxicating moments for the teacher and, often, for students, and when these moments occur the teacher is uplifted, reassured, and inspired. This is even more the feeling when teachers get students to see these important moments as part of a longer process, when students begin to see where their learning and efforts might take them. Something changes when learning takes on the character of a project students want to carry out. At every turn something new and different is experienced or understood, and learning gets deeper and more meaningful. Students like thinking about subject matter things, and they like who they become *when* they think about these things.

This is the ultimate victory for the teacher—when students fully *identify with* a particular discipline. We can think, for instance, of the middle or high school student who gives him or herself over to a given subject or academic discipline—the young man who signs up for every available music class or musical group, for example, or the young woman who falls in love with science and takes every class the school offers. These are students who in answering the deepest, most sincere self-identity question—the existential "Who am I?" question every self-aware human being eventually asks—may answer at least in part with reference to their love of an academic discipline. "I am someone who knows and loves music (or history, or science, or anthropology)." "I am a reader of important literature." "I am someone who cannot live without art." For just about everyone, this love of a discipline, and this kind of self-identity, starts in school—in some classroom, with some teacher, being involved in the activities of a particular discipline.

Beyond this is an even deeper and more profound answer to the self-identity question that also starts in school. That's the answer that shares something with how a philosopher or theologian might answer the self-identity question—the person who seeks after the truth of things, someone who cannot settle for false answers or opinions about things but who through rational inquiry or a studied leap of faith seeks the ground of all understanding. This answer underscores the work of rationality—of understanding, of exploring and thinking through essential questions—and this almost always starts in the apprenticeship of academic disciplines. That is, it starts with that same school, that same teacher, working carefully but ever more deeply into the ideas contained in some curriculum.

The Socrates we see in the Platonic dialogues gives us the highest model of this kind of club membership—the Socrates who presses his interlocutors to give up their false understandings about the things they are discussing but who then entreats them to stay with him as full partners in seeking after the truth of things. It isn't always possible for K–12 students to catch-up to the knowledge and understanding of their teachers and so be continuing partners in inquiry, but there are moments when students and their teacher can find something of an equal footing and discover things together as co-inquirers "into the truth of things." The best part of being an English teacher, for instance, is when students observe something in a poem or other literary work that the teacher has never noticed before—something that changes or deepens the teacher's understanding of the work. A good student question in a history, math, or science class—or even in a first or third grade classroom—can bring into view for the teacher and her students a certain aspect of the subject matter the teacher hadn't before considered. That's what happens in academic clubs when everyone participates.

We can begin to see how this metaphor casts a very different light on teaching and learning (and teachers and schools) than is cast when reformers speak the language of the economic and consumership gods and talk about learning as being about "power" or "life options." In this newer light, learning is not an addition problem—it is a journey, or a project taken on for very personal reasons. Learning is a question of who you are or who you are becoming through your learning. Learning is not merely something you endure so you can eventually secure material benefits. The primary task of the teacher is to pull students into this community, not to "add value" to what students know in some prescribed and measureable way. Curriculum standards still apply and the subject matter or content doesn't change. But standards aren't gods commanding obsequiousness from teachers, and neither is academic content so formal or cold. The meaningfulness of content is what's most important to the teacher. That's because the teacher knows students buy into club membership when they begin to see why the subject should matter to them. They buy into club membership when they see a good reason for learning.

Possible Weaknesses of the "Club" Metaphor

These are noble and inspired images of teaching and learning, and the metaphor of the "club" speaks to what every teacher wants: to see students earnestly pursuing the learning offered to them. Still, this seems a little too optimistic. Can we expect all students to love everything they are taught—or, to follow the metaphor, to want to be fully fledged members of every learning club?

In *What is Education?* Philip Jackson acknowledges these limitations on the enthusiasms of students.[5] Not every student is going to love everything put in front of him or her by a teacher. Yet, Jackson argues, every teacher should aspire to having every school subject *matter* at least minimally to every student. And it should matter, he argues, not just for instrumental reasons—for attaining high grades, or winning the teacher's approval, or even opening doors to higher aspirations. It should matter for *intrinsic* reasons.[6] That is, it must matter to students personally—they need to see some essential part of themselves being made in, or reflected in, the subject matter. Still, our club metaphor dims some as we admit there will be fringe members, or part-time members, populating our learning clubs.

Also, as the metaphor draws our attention toward what is possible or most ideal in school situations, we may fail to realize and carefully consider the tougher, less idyllic side of learning. Learning doesn't always have the glow of minds locked together, fascinated by some glorious aspect of the subject matter. Sometimes it looks more like hard work. It means practicing skills over and over, mastering the vocabulary of the discourse, recognizing key events or people, doing problem sets until you really understand a concept. This is part of club membership, too—the dirty work, if you will, without which there is no true participation in a discipline.

Still, the club metaphor holds—it remains valid and useful. It describes, in a general way, the hopes and intentions of the first grade teacher who straightens out a student's recital of the ABC's just as it describes the hopes and intentions of the physics teacher who, like Socrates with his interlocutors, gathers her students together to wrestle with large and invigorating questions. But the metaphor would benefit from a more thorough description of teachers in classrooms—especially a description of the kinds of "hopes and intentions" classroom teachers (and Socrates) seem to have. As we find language to describe these hopes and intentions, or the purpose for learning that is revealed in what teachers do, we develop a deeper and more profound understanding of teaching. And we come closer to finding genuine reasons to learn that will encourage more students to "join the club." For help in seeing the purpose of learning common to the tasks of teachers, we turn to the book referred to above, Philip Jackson's *What is Education?*

Education and the Path to "Perfection"

Jackson suggests teachers "traffic in truths"—a lovely metaphor, too, to describe what teachers do—and one that suggests we're looking at purposes, not a survey of teaching techniques. According to Jackson, teachers deal in factual truths (basic information about something), systematic truths (clusters of notions associated with particular concepts in a discipline), instrumental truths (ideas about how to do things), and moral truths (truths about how to live one's life, especially truths about relationships we encounter in our lives). And there is one other kind of truth. Jackson calls these last and critically important truths in which teachers traffic *subjective truths*. The teacher's concern here is what students themselves take up as true—what they take to be true about themselves, about others, and about the world in general. This, Jackson says, is what teachers consciously seek to establish or modify through their teaching. Teachers must bring all the truths in which they traffic to life for students—to "make them accessible, interesting, and perhaps even vital to those at the receiving end of that transaction." The subjective truth involves getting students to possess fully what knowledge the teacher transmits, to get students to accept it, to take ownership of it.[7]

The overriding reason for education—what Jackson calls the ultimate mission of education—is to extend rationality.[8] This is what happens when teachers traffic in these different truths—when, for instance, the elementary teachers teach students how to add, subtract, multiply, and divide numbers, and the high school world history teacher teaches about ancient Greek and Roman civilizations. The elementary teachers give students mathematical skills, certainly, but they also begin to initiate students into mathematical concepts and mathematical modes of thinking about the world. The world history teacher offers information about the Greeks and Romans, but even more important are moral truths and the systematic truths about history and historical thinking. These truths extend students' rationality—assuming, of course, that students accept these truths, that they take them up subjectively.

We see teachers trafficking in truths and extending the rationality of students just about any time we peek into a teacher's classroom. We see this effort as a teacher endeavors to shape the thinking of his or her students. Jackson suggests that "thought is always on the move," especially in a class-room.[9] Thought drifts, and wanders, and flits from one thing to another, and one of the main tasks of the teacher is to keep the thoughts of students channeled and focused. Jackson notes that thought, when disciplined, moves predominantly along three tracks: horizontal, vertical, and ellipti-cal. Thought moves horizontally as new information, ideas, or knowledge is added to what is already known. It moves vertically—either "up" or "deep-er"—in search of a universal or ultimate explanation of something. Ellipti-cal thought goes out in search of an explanation of things, then returns to qualify or correct those explanations. Most lessons teachers offer their students invite or require one or more of these movements of thought. Thought is always being exercised in classrooms.

But, of course, students often make mistakes in their thinking. Based on what they see or hear from students, every good teacher has an instinct for how to bridge the gap from where students are in their understanding of what is being taught to where students need to go next in their think-ing or understanding. At least in part, this involves teachers recognizing student errors or misconceptions and knowing how to respond to them— how to correct the mistakes and clarify misconceptions without damaging the student's often fragile ego and even more fragile commitment to the endeavor. Jackson invokes Hegel's use of the German word *Aufhebung* to describe a fundamental pedagogical move of teachers. *Aufhebung* describes the exchange between the teacher and her students that is both *appreciative* and *critical*—the kind of comment that both encourages students and challenges them:

> The teacher responding in a speculative mode says things like, "That's a very good point, Sarah, but have you considered..." or "I certainly agree with you, Fred, but I wonder..." or "Wow. I would never have thought of that myself, Mark. Good for you! But would you say..." Each response from the teacher is intended to be supportive and encouraging while clearly signaling the limits of every attempt to reach the truth in some final sense.[10]

We note that these exchanges do not totally reject the remark or answer the student has made. Some real part of that remark is kept or preserved. It is even honored as an advance in thinking about the idea at hand. Yet, while some part of what the student has offered is preserved, that same remark is, at the same time, cancelled or rendered invalid or incomplete. The last of this three-step process (captured here only with the ellipses) is the part that seeks to elevate the thinking or understanding of the student. The initial remark of the student has some truth to it, but is incomplete or incorrect. What would we need to understand or say if we were to comprehend this idea more fully? *Cancel* what is incorrect in the offered statement; *preserve* what is true about it; *elevate* the thinking to a higher level—the three parts of *Aufhebung*, and the three parts of a basic interchange pattern between teacher and student.

This three-part pattern is exercised not only verbally as in Jackson's example, above, but in other ways as well. A mathematics teacher working with a student on a geometric proof will show the student what she did right, get her to see what she did wrong, and help her know what she needs to do next. The English teacher will, either in writing or verbally, praise the part of a student's essay that is wonderful, offer helpful criticisms on the parts that don't work so well, and get the student to think how he might say more. This three-part "dance" is also, as Jackson notes, what we do when we think privately about things—when a teacher is nowhere around. When we find imperfections in our understanding of something, we admit to ourselves what is mistaken in our thinking, keep what we still believe is true about what we understand, and try to reach for something more clear and definite. *Aufhebung* is not just a customary pedagogical move; it is the fundamental movement of reason.[11] In classrooms, this is a move to extend rationality.

We can see the trafficking in truth, the movements of thought, and this three part pedagogical move of teachers, Jackson says, as being among the "mundane" tasks of teaching. That is, they are the routine things every teacher must do when students learn something new. But if we think more carefully about these tasks, we are entitled to think about them in more "lofty" terms, Jackson argues—that is, as pointing toward an ideal or essential understanding of education even as they do, indeed, describe the everyday experience of education.[12] Even in the everyday things we do in the classroom we can sense something about the end or the ideal we seek with students—something well beyond what we actually do in classrooms or can describe in curriculum standards, curriculum goals, or learning objectives. We are not usually able to put our finger on just what that ideal is, and we don't always have time to ponder it, but we can often sense it or feel it.

Our trafficking in truth with students, Jackson argues, points upward. "It points upward," he says, "toward the pinnacle of human striving and even beyond. By prompting us to exceed our limits, it aims higher than we can go. The effort it initiates and sustains leads to our making the best use of whatever powers of thought and feeling it calls into action."[13] Jackson names the end, or destination, to which we would, or might, arrive if we kept going upward. And it is, indeed, a lofty destination. It is "perfection."

But this requires some explanation.

The Perfection We Seek for Students

Jackson gives us a fresh way of seeing moments of learning, and we can see something like perfection as a goal in even the simplest among them. We see it, for instance, when a first grader finally realizes that $2 + 2$ really does equal 4 instead of some other number. At that moment she has, indeed, made a small step toward something we might call perfection. That student has acquired a truth—in this case, a factual truth—and as she moves on in mathematics (and all other areas) she acquires many more factual truths. And she acquires systematic, instrumental, and moral truths. Her thoughts move horizontally, vertically, and elliptically. Every time a teacher preserves, cancels, and elevates something in her thinking, she gets something corrected and improved, and she moves closer to perfection. She extends her rationality. If she accepts and embraces more truths in the learning possibilities she is offered, she begins to step into the full flush of her intellectual powers. She takes up deeper, more affecting, and more abiding truths in everything she studies, and in doing this she is made better than she was. She is made more "perfect" than she would otherwise have been.

This tells us about the moment of learning not as the cognitive scientist or empirical researcher want to describe it. This description doesn't tell us what the brain is doing at the moment of learning, and it doesn't hypothesize about what teaching methods work best to guarantee learning. It certainly has nothing to say about the uses of education—the economic power or life options learning might bring with it. But Jackson's insights resonate with us both as teachers and learners. They capture something we believe is essential about what happens and where we are going when we learn. Perfection *does* seem to be the destination. The problem is we can't seem to say exactly what we mean by the perfection we seem to be seeking. We can describe the little steps we take along the path to perfection—our getting mathematical concepts straight in our heads, for instance. It seems we can describe concrete features of perfection but cannot describe its essence. That essence lies outside of us, somehow.

Jackson suggests the ideal of perfection lies outside *all* our endeavors. All disciplines and modes of thinking about the world—from art, religion, philosophy, morals, the sciences, and scholarly studies in general—share a family resemblance. "Each points toward the unattainable," Jackson argues. "The dedicated practitioners in each of those domains aspires to a level of perfection that lies forever out of reach."[14] Having the freedom to ask, question, probe, and discover in their particular domains—having, that is, the freedom to follow the dictates of reason itself—these practitioners do not merely articulate the truths they currently find, and they do more, even, than offer explanations that tell *why* such things are true. According to Jackson, these practitioners have a target, or an end point, that points toward the *totality* of truth with respect to their particular domains. That totality, which is the target, is beyond the empirical truths these practitioners have found and can explain. The truths we know today point toward a truth that transcends reality—a truth we may never know or articulate. But it's there. We seek it. It gives point and direction to our actual efforts, even if we can't completely say what it is.[15]

Education, Jackson believes, deserves to be included in "that distinguished company of seekers after perfection," and he expects that "almost all professional educators would agree."[16] If this is true, then as artists, philosophers, or theologians reach toward the truth in their domains—the truth that is out of their reach—so do educators reach in the domain of education. With and for our students, we gesture toward, or move toward, the end point—what Jackson calls perfection—without being able to explain that perfection. In this, educators are caused to think about the *essence* of education—that is, what education is *essentially*.[17]

Clubs, Truths, Perfection—and Reasons to Learn

So far, then, we have come to the idea of "perfection" in our argument—a provocative idea, and one that lets us connect the efforts of all teachers, from the first grade teacher to Socrates. The little pedagogical moves classroom teachers make, like correcting student mistakes, and the larger and more captivating learning tasks they also offer—all move students in the direction of their perfection. But so far we have not said much about how all this will help us answer the demand of the student who wants to know why he has to learn a particular skill or master a particular idea. That is, it may not seem we are any closer to giving students good reasons to learn. But perhaps we are not so far away as we might think.

It makes a certain kind of intuitive sense to compare starting to learn something with being initiated into a club. There is a group of people (represented in classrooms primarily by the teacher) and these people know how to do something, or they understand something, or they appreciate something—and learning involves coming to be able to do what they do, understand what they understand, and appreciate what they appreciate. The teacher and the other people in these clubs must like what they do when they are doing club activities. Those activities must be meaningful to them. There must be something there worth doing or understanding otherwise those people wouldn't stay as members of that club. But what is it that's so compelling or meaningful in each of these clubs? What is it about mathematics that's so compelling? Or science? Or reading and thinking about great literature? Or the other clubs?

What is so interesting and compelling about these clubs must be found, at least in part, in and among the factual, systematic, instrumental and moral truths in which teachers traffic. As the teacher helps students focus their thoughts horizontally, vertically, and elliptically, students explore these truths, and with this students begin to see why the teacher and other club members find the subject matter so meaningful. The students are brought closer to this understanding, potentially, every time the teacher preserves, cancels, then elevates their thinking. Sometimes all this is immediately rewarding to students and their teacher, and sometimes there is significant work involved. We usually measure the progress and direction of these student efforts by noting improvements, but we can also see the progress as a move toward perfection.

Jackson reveals the central drama between teachers and students—whether or not students will *subjectively* accept the truths the teacher is offering—that is, whether or not students find these things interesting or important, and whether or not they take them up, possess them, and are changed by them. Like Smith, Jackson doesn't tell us how to do that. Neither author gives us a list of techniques guaranteed to grab the attention and care of students. But if neither author offers a list of techniques, they do make one thing clear: the solution is in the subject matter itself. There is *something* in that subject matter that draws in devotees of that club. There is in mathematics, or biology, or literature, or any of the other subject fields, something powerful for us—something that might move us, or change us, or improve us—something that might give us eyes to see our world and ourselves differently. If students can begin to feel and know the power of that subject matter, they are much more likely to stick with their study of it. They will want to know more. They will want to become full-fledged club members, and they will come to possess truths of the discipline. Eventually, the perfection that beckons to the mathematician, to the physicist, and to other practitioners will begin to beckon to students. That's at least the ideal teachers are given to try to realize with and for students. That's the draw of the subject matter. That's the reason to learn.

Considering the Realities of Teaching

There is, all at the same time, something exciting, daunting, and problematic about thinking in this rather large and abstract way about reasons teachers can give students to learn. This way of thinking about teaching and learning is exciting, first of all, because it seems to promise rich, complex, and compelling thinking that teachers and students can share together in classrooms. To get students to take up and be moved by the same provocative questions that real musicians, historians, chemists, psychologists (etc.) have come to understand, and *still* try to understand—that's powerful stuff. The history teacher who brings these truths to life in the classroom will have a better answer to give to students when they ask why they need to study history than "Because history repeats itself"—that tired, true, and meaningless answer students are used to hearing. And the mathematics teacher will have more to say than "So we can figure out how many cans of paint we'll need to paint the living room." Such answers are abysmal, no matter how true they may be, and they never convince students to want to give themselves over to the study of history, mathematics, or any other discipline. The "because you'll need it in college" reason is just as bad or worse.

But there are several daunting parts to this thinking, especially the worry about how we will get students to do more than simply be aware of, and be vaguely interested in, these large and compelling questions and issues. Students aren't supposed to just "feel the emotion" of certain ideas. They are supposed to acquire specific knowledge, skills, and understandings and begin to participate in the discipline in some real and genuine way. They're supposed to master some part of the discipline.

And, of course, certain problems come to mind. It's a little easier for the high school teacher to see how the "big questions" can become central to his or her teaching at that level, but how does this work for elementary and middle school teachers? The end-point of perfection or subject-specific truths seems awfully far away for these teachers. And how can any teacher worry about such an end-point when standards spell out more than the teacher can possibly teach and standardized tests loom at the end of the year? Especially when some narrow-minded, number-crunching administrator or reformer just wants to count-up what students have learned so he or she can compute some "value" score and determine which teachers get to keep their jobs.

We must, it seems, continue to look "up" to these abstract ideas we're talking about while also considering how these ideas can be managed—how they can be made real and doable for the classroom teacher. And we must make these noble purposes into reasons for learning that will satisfy students.

Reasons to Learn: Ancient Ideals and Essential Questions

Howard Gardner wrestles with how to talk about these big, abstract ideas in *The Disciplined Mind: Beyond Facts and Standardized Tests, The K–12 Education that Every Child Deserves*[18] and in his more recent *Truth, Beauty, and Goodness Reframed: Educating for the Virtues in the Twenty-first Century.*[19] Gardner traffics in the biggest and most abstract of the philosophical ideas of interest to Socrates, Plato, and the rest of the Greek philosophers—the good, the true, and the beautiful—even as he makes clear he is not a Platonist who believes we can reason our way to a single and absolute understanding of these ideas. The ancients saw the good, the true, and the beautiful as critical personal virtues—virtues it was important for the Greek city-state to nurture in its citizens, especially its young.

To speak of the good, the true, and the beautiful—and even the idea of virtue itself—is exceedingly problematic in our day and age, as Gardner realizes. But still these ideas have some resonance with us. We want the young to avoid the clearly false, ugly and evil even if we cannot always agree about what is true, or beautiful, or good. Gardner writes:

> [E]ducation must *continue* to confront truth (falsity), beauty (ugliness), and goodness (evil), in full awareness of the problematic facets of these categories and the disagreements across cultures and subcultures. The concerns may be ancient, but they must be perennially revisited and refashioned. And the academic disciplines remain the best way to pursue this mission.[20]

Teachers can pursue study of these virtues by organizing careful examinations of particular instances of good or evil, truth or falsity, and beauty or ugliness. Countless events or objects might be found and productively studied, and Gardner offers three as examples in the text. In the realm of good and evil, Gardner chooses the Holocaust, especially the Wannsee conference, held January 20, 1942, when leaders of the Nazi Third Reich gathered together to think about how to solve the "Jewish problem"; in the realm of beauty and ugliness, a scene in the first act of Mozart's opera *The Mar-*

riage of Figaro, where a trio of singers, each with his or her own competing agenda and melody line, move the plot of the complicated opera forward in an amazing and beautiful way; in the realm of truth and falsity, a look at evolution by studying Darwin's discovery of the different finches on the Galapagos Islands off the coast of Ecuador.[21]

There are certainly facts to organize in the study of such things, and skills to acquire, and understandings to master—and there would no doubt be any number of "standards" teachers could check-off along the way. But Gardner makes it clear that the big questions of goodness, beauty, and truth are to animate the study of these or similar topics. Human beings cannot seem to leave questions about goodness, truth, and beauty alone—people in every time and place in our history seek to know what these things, and their opposites, really are. Or, they can believe they embrace and embody what is good, true, and beautiful, but be tragically wrong, and instead embrace what is evil, false, or ugly. Gardner wants "essential questions" about such things to be at the heart of what is studied and learned in school:

> I personally favor a "pathway for understanding." Let me indicate just one of its dimensions. Education in this pathway ought to be inspired by a set of *essential questions*: Who are we? Where do we come from? What do we consider to be true or false, beautiful or ugly, good or evil? What is the fate of the earth? How do we fit in? What is the earth made of? What are we made of? Why do we live, and why do we die? Are our destinies under the control of God or some other "higher power"? What is love? What is hatred? Why do we make war? Must we? What is justice and how can we achieve it?[22] (emphasis in the original)

Such questions, Gardner argues, are the real "stuff" of the disciplines. The task of the teacher is to offer students access to the best answers to these human questions:

> [T]he rationale and the reward for studying the disciplines should be enhanced access to, and stronger purchase on, the major questions of human life. If you want to understand what it means to be alive, study biology; if you want to understand the composition and dynamic of the physical world, study chemistry, physics, or geology; if you want to understand your own background, study national history and immigration patterns and experiences; if you want to gain intimate knowledge of the feats of which human beings are capable, study and participate in art, science, religion, athletics, and perhaps even developmental psychology.[23]

Gardner does not outline exactly how the study of Mozart's opera, the Wannsee conference, or Darwin's finches should proceed. And while he clearly intends the study of such things to be thorough and deep, he doesn't recommend a particular length of study. Should this be what teachers would call a "unit" of study, lasting two or three weeks? Should it be longer, maybe even a mini-course, or full course? How does the teacher tasked with "covering" a multitude of topics in a year-long history course, for instance, justify spending extended time on the Wannsee conference—not the whole Holocaust, mind you, but just (or primarily) the Wannsee conference?

These are important questions teachers must answer. But what teachers can't do is let certain real complications of organizing curriculum take away their "upward" vision—the vision that sees these essential human questions. And, too often, this is what happens. Study of the Holocaust becomes a quick survey of names, dates, and places in a larger unit about World War II; evolution becomes a unit to dispense with quickly before certain parents have time enough to mount a complaint; a music survey course has so much ground to cover that an extended look at any single piece of music becomes impossible. And so essential questions often go unasked in the curriculum. The history class never takes up the question of hatred, justice, or the goodness or evil of man. The science class talks (ad nauseum) about the scientific method, but never gets students to realize the kinds and magnitude of truth that science articulates and how those truths compete or are in tension with other kinds of truth. The music class never elevates or sophisticates the taste of students.

Gardner wants students to struggle with essential questions—if not in regard to the Holocaust, the Wannsee conference, or Mozart's opera, then in regard to something else equally revealing. And here we can connect Gardner's interest in essential questions with the argument Jackson makes about perfection. Gardner's hope that students will learn to seek goodness over evil, beauty over ugliness, and truth over falsity sounds more than a little bit like Jackson's argument that perfectibility is the end-point of education. Students who question and learn to seek what is higher and best in their lives and in culture instead of what is lower and worse inch toward their own perfection. And Gardner's explanation of how academic disciplines examine essential questions—the major questions of human life—helps us understand what Jackson might mean when he suggests that practitioners of scholarly disciplines "aspire to a level of perfection that lies forever out of reach." Mozart reached for pure and unadorned beauty in composing *The Marriage of Figaro* just as Darwin reached for pure and unadorned truth in crafting the theory of evolution, but neither man achieved what he sought. The Nazi's went straight toward evil, though they could justify their actions, at least to themselves. That's why Gardner calls for a careful study of the Wannsee conference and not merely a showing of a movie like *Schindler's List.* That unbelievably powerful movie shapes and encourages the moral and emotional response we should have to the tragedy and travesty of the Holocaust. But it is the careful work of the historian (and others) in looking at every aspect of that pivotal Nazi conference that helps us understand how one group of people can look beyond precepts of good and evil to justify a considered and purposeful massacre of another group of people. And that's a lesson worth learning.

In looking "up" to these abstract ideals while thinking about real and vital human events, we understand what attracts practitioners of these scholarly endeavors—including teachers and, hopefully, their students—to academic clubs. The clubs promise serious study of serious things—things that raise essential human questions that have always plagued and intrigued us. When we orient our teaching toward these questions in interesting and purposeful ways, we give students the highest and most compelling reasons to learn—to take seriously and stay with their studies.

Reasons to Learn: Human Hopes, Fears, and Passions

We are now some distance away from the gods of Economic Utility and Consumerism that Postman says we have typically put before students as reasons for learning. Gardner doesn't entice students to learn by promising them that if they pay attention and do what they are told they can get a good job and buy all the good stuff they want. He doesn't promise them "power" and he doesn't promise them "life options." He believes teachers can really get students to think seriously about essential questions—about things like the Wannsee conference, or Darwin's finches, or Mozart's opera. Thinking about profound human questions sounds like a much better and truer reason to learn than do the low economic reasons we continue to trumpet. But we need to say more about how teachers might make this happen. And we must not forget about the elementary and middle school teachers whose students aren't ready to confront the big questions Darwin, the Holocaust, and Mozart pose for us. What can these teachers find in this kind of reason to learn that will work for them?

Here, Kieran Egan's book *An Imaginative Approach to Teaching* offers us some help.[24] Egan argues that teachers, at all levels, need to involve their students emotionally in the subject matter they are to study. The following is from the Introduction to his book:

> Students don't need a throbbing passion for learning algebra or a swooning joy in learning about punctuation, but successful education does require

some emotional involvement of the students with the subject matter. All knowledge is human knowledge and all knowledge is a product of human hopes, fears, and passions. To bring knowledge to life in students' minds we must introduce it to students in the context of human hopes, fears, and passions in which it finds its fullest meaning.[25]

Egan's suggestion that students don't need "a throbbing passion" or "a swooning joy" for the different things we give them to learn ought, first of all, to bring a kind of relief to teachers. We can relate this to the three curricular examples suggested by Gardner. No one should expect even a single student to walk into class with a throbbing passion to study the Wannsee conference, or Darwin's finches, or Mozart's opera. We would also not expect every middle school student to have such a passion about magnets, geography, the parts of a short story, or other things he is given to learn. Neither would all elementary students have such passions for things offered by their teachers. Yet, none of these teachers is foiled in their attempts to get students to study particular things just because students are initially blasé about or seemingly uninterested in possible study—providing, that is, that these teachers can find some way to involve students *emotionally* in the study of things they offer. That involvement becomes possible when teachers identify the human hopes, fears, and passions at the heart of the thing to be studied—hopes, fears, or passions teachers can get students to feel or realize within themselves.

Before teaching a lesson, or before putting a lesson together for students, teachers need to worry less about their blasé and recalcitrant students than they need to worry about themselves. That is, before the history teacher worries about what will captivate his or her students about the bombing of Hiroshima, or the math teacher about what will get students to pay attention to the Pythagorean Theorem, the teacher needs to think through his or her own response to that piece of the subject matter. Teachers need to ask themselves, Egan suggests, if they understand what is at stake in this thing they are about to teach—why it is so meaningful and important to them, as individuals and as a member of the "club" that is supposed to take these things seriously. The teacher needs to find or rediscover what it is in this subject matter that evokes wonder, what it is that is emotionally engaging, for him or her. The teacher needs to articulate this, then find a way to put it at the center of the lesson.

So, then, to use one of our examples from above: If I am a science teacher and it is time for me to teach about evolution, I have some thinking to do. First, I need to think of what grips *me* about this topic—what it is that is so compelling that I *must* think about it. What is it of "human hopes, fears, and passions" that is in this story of Darwin and his finches? What was driving Darwin in this direction? What moving human question was he trying to answer, and to what extent should all of us be moved by this question? And, here, stealing the language written in the curriculum guides, the science standards, or the science textbook doesn't count for much. We're not looking for the bland language of lesson objectives or the over-edited language of the textbook. We're looking for the heartfelt language spoken by a lover of a discipline. What is it in the intentions, obstacles, skills, insights, and accomplishments of Darwin—and what of the human, scientific, social, and even religious lessons and repercussions of his discovery—do I find so remarkable and worthy of my thought and understanding? That's what I first need to come to grips with, and I need to have faith that if these things are compelling for me to think about, they can be made compelling for my students to think about, too. My students, through my teaching, can come to understand and value some or all of what I have valued.

The middle school geography teacher needs to ask the same kinds of questions about the lesson she is going to offer her seventh grade students about maps, or some other topic—and so does the elementary teacher about what she teaches. What is emotionally engaging about the topic? How is it meaningful? Why should it matter to us? Does the topic have something "heroic" about it? What people, or what ideas, connected to this topic make it full of wonder for us?

It isn't hard to see what kinds of questions the middle school geography teacher might think about when considering the lesson she is preparing on maps. What human hope, fear, or passion would lead someone to think of making a map of some place? When was the first map written? How many different kinds of maps are there? How old is the oldest map, and how does it differ from maps we see today? What difference have maps made in the course of human history? Who made the first map—and should he (or she) be a kind of hero to us? Do maps themselves have something "heroic" about them in their scope, their exactitude, in what they make possible for us? These are questions, first of all, for the teacher. But it isn't hard to see how they would work to make the study of maps *emotionally meaningful* for middle school students as they begin their study. If these aren't quite Gardner's essential questions, they are certainly akin to them.

It's the same thing for the second grade teacher trying to find ways to engage her students emotionally as they learn about place value. Place value had to come from somewhere. There had to be a reason for it—something of human hopes, fears, and passions that made it inevitable. Place value solves a serious counting problem for us. What story could teachers tell to get students to see why place value is necessary and how it works without merely plunging students into the mechanics of it all? What would engage the imagination of students enough that they could almost "see it" before they can even do it? Egan works through this particular example in great detail in his book.[26] The second grade teacher needs to identify what is wonderful about place value, not just break down the different skills and understandings students will have to master.

Egan offers "frameworks" for thinking about how to craft lessons. The frameworks he sketches are constructed around the *cognitive tools* human beings have at their disposal at different stages in their development. Younger children (ones who do not yet know how to read) still have a whole host of cognitive tools. They know how to hear and appreciate stories, for example. They have language skills enough to enjoy, understand, and even create jokes and metaphors. They can organize their thinking around binary opposites—hot/cold, sad/happy, good/evil—a first version of the more sophisticated opposites we see in Gardner's discussion of good and evil, truth and falsity, beautiful and ugly. Children this age love rhyme, rhythm, and pattern, and gossip, play, and mystery are all things they are equipped to learn from and enjoy. These are tools for learning, and they are tools that help students connect emotionally with what they are given to learn.[27]

The literate middle school student has an additional set of cognitive tools that can help him connect emotionally when the social studies teacher decides it's time for the study of maps. At this age and stage of development, students give themselves heroes to worship, and they love to think about extremes of experience and reality. They would be fascinated if the teacher could show them the oldest map, the largest map, the strangest map, and how GPS devices work as maps. They have a natural sense of wonder, love even longer and more complicated stories, and naturally tend to collect things. The teacher who uses and appeals to these and other cognitive tools helps students of this age come to see why the study of maps (or any other topic) should matter to them.[28]

Most older students have cognitive tools more attuned to theoretical thinking. They can (and want to) reach for more abstract ideas. They have a newly found sense of agency—both more independent, yet more deeply related to things that shape their world. Challenging authority and truth is a passion with them, and that energy can be channeled into investigating general laws and ideas in particular disciplines. They can appreciate general truths and find contradictions or anomalies—the kind of elliptical thinking Jackson talks about. These are tools that can be used to engross students in the study of important matters, if teachers but appeal to them.[29]

Conclusion

It was Mr. Peters, at the end of Chapter 6, with his sense that the "Knowledge is Power" sign hanging in his classroom wasn't sending the right moral message to his students who sent us in search of better reasons to learn. Let's blame him for the rather long excursion we have taken in this chapter.

We have been exploring what Mr. Peters wanted to articulate: the better, deeper richer, and more nuanced reasons we have for students to learn and to care about their learning. There is something in what we teach students that is infinitely valuable to them—something that can make every difference to the lives they are to lead, something that may have to do with future earnings, power, and life options, but something that is well beyond such things. That something has to do with who we are as human beings, with our self-identity. What is it that we get in schools that makes a difference in the person we become—an essential, vital difference? The person who really, genuinely *has* a subject matter, or several subject matters—the person who possesses musical abilities or sensibilities, or the person who has the openness and hunger to possess great literature, or the person who has the habits and curiosities of the scientist—these people have something that brings real joy, perspective, and understanding to their lives. Their lives are changed by what they have. They are "in the club" of people who know, understand and appreciate that subject matter. They readily traffic in the truths of what they know and continue to learn. They are ready for more horizontal, vertical, and elliptical thinking. Their rationality is extended. They are closer to perfect even if they don't really know the perfection that is possible for them. They are ready, in many ways, to take on questions of truth and falsity, good and bad, beauty and ugliness. Or, at the very least, they see these questions in the issues and concerns they see in the world or face in their lives. If they are not ready to be a full participant in working through important questions, they are at least able to value and profit from those who do.

If we are at all optimistic about the students in our schools—if we believe even disenchanted older students or students in tough circumstances haven't lost all the curiosity, the imagination, or the desire to know that we have always attributed to human beings—then we can, with Gardner and Egan, think of how to get to and set those springs of learning. If the Wannsee conference, Darwin's finches, or Mozart's opera aren't the things that will captivate a certain group of students, then we'll choose others. But we'll have faith that students will see why they must thoroughly think through what we've chosen—that there is something vital for all of us to know and realize, something that sheds light on other issues in our lives. We'll see something of human hopes, fears, and passions in everything we study—even place value, or maps, or Roman history. When students begin to see even "drab and boring" pieces of subject matter as the product of real human hopes, fears, and passions they can understand and share, we have a hold on their interests and commitments that we don't have when we force them to learn primarily out of fear—fear of grades, fear of the standardized test, fear of not getting into college, fear of not having good life options. We can stop telling students to learn "Because I said so," and "Because it's going to be on the test." We can help students see better and richer reasons to learn than mere economic power and social position, even as we don't rule such things out. We need no longer utter weak, ineffective, awful and corrupt reasons to learn in our classrooms.

We can also talk in better and richer ways about the two other indictments made against teachers that we explored in Chapter 6—that teachers don't work hard enough and aren't very effective. Hard work isn't measured by how long the lights stay on in the teacher's classroom every night after school, and effectiveness isn't primarily measured by end-of-the-year test scores, no matter what reformers and the numerically-inclined among us may want to believe. Effort and effectiveness aren't measured so much as they are observed and witnessed when we watch teachers and students together in classrooms. The ideas of Smith, Jackson, Gardner, and Egan give us ways of talking about what we want to see from teachers working with students. Effort and effectiveness are both apparent when we see teachers pulling students "into the club" of their subject matters. We see it when everything that is said in the classroom and every routine and practice—from grading, to kinds of assignments, to pedagogical choices—invites students into the club instead of slamming the clubhouse door in their faces. We see effort and can expect effectiveness when teachers ask that first and most important question: What is it that I find so meaningful and emotionally engaging about this topic or idea I'm about to teach? Effort is finding the real human hopes, fears, and passions that lie behind the particular aspect of a teacher's subject matter—an aspect that can otherwise look disconnected, arbitrary, and unimportant to students. We know a teacher has been effective when we see students take-up and seriously consider one or more of the essential questions that lie at the heart of a subject matter. We see effort and effectiveness when teachers gracefully preserve for students what they do well, show them where they have made a misstep, and elevate their thinking or work. We want to see rising student test scores as a measure of teaching effectiveness. But we know we see the kind of teacher we want our children to have when everything the teacher does for students is a step toward completing those students—a step toward their possible perfection.

Conversation about teacher effort, teacher effectiveness, and the purposes we are trying to achieve with students should center on these kinds of things. These are not the only important conversations we need to have—we can talk about student test scores, and we can talk about effective schools research, too. And we need to talk about all the issues reformers are reluctant to talk about—things like getting students and their families all the goods and services they need in order to survive and thrive. But the issues raised in this chapter about the need to give students good reasons to learn, and ways to do that, are crucial if we really want to improve teaching and learning in our schools. Furthermore, this is the talk that is natural to teachers. It's what they think about all the time. You can't stand in front of 30 sometimes expectant, sometimes sulking, sometimes tired, and sometimes wild students and *not* wonder how you can give them a good reason to learn. But shouting at teachers about meeting standards, and raising test scores, and making sure they show adequate "growth scores" doesn't help teachers think about these things. And neither does insinuating that they don't work hard enough or care enough. These things just get in the way.

Of course, we're having no such conversations in schools or in the public at large—or such conversations are isolated and private. And that's largely the fault of educational reformers and so many others who have taken over the public discourse about schools. That discourse, as I have suggested throughout this book, starts and ends with the blaming of teachers. It is talk that is narrow, shallow, and full of resentment—and it is talk that will never improve teaching and learning in schools in ways that will really make a difference.

Notes

1. Frank Smith, *The Book of Learning and Forgetting* (New York, NY: Teachers College Press, 1998), 11.
2. Ibid., 11–12.
3. Ibid., 18.
4. Ibid., 60–65.
5. Philip Jackson, *What is Education?* (Chicago: University of Chicago Press, 2012).
6. Ibid., 56.
7. Ibid., 16–19.
8. Ibid., 28.
9. Ibid., 23–26.
10. Ibid., 31.
11. Ibid., 34.

12. Ibid., 44–47. I am drawing attention to what Jackson calls the "essence" and the "experience" of education—or the ideal and the real—on only a small part of Jackson's argument. The interplay of the essence and the experience of education is the subject of the entire book.

13. Ibid., 45.

14. Ibid., 62.

15. Ibid., 66.

16. Ibid., 62.

17. Ibid., 69.

18. Howard Gardner, *The Disciplined Mind: Beyond Facts and Standardized Tests, the K–12 Education that Every Child Deserves* (New York, NY: Penguin Books, 2000).

19. Howard Gardner, *Truth, Beauty, and Goodness Reframed: Educating for the Virtues in the Twenty-first Century* (New York, NY: Basic Books, 2011).

20. Gardner, *The Disciplined Mind*, 35.

21. Ibid., 138–141.

22. Ibid., 216.

23. Ibid., 218.

24. Kieran Egan, *An Imaginative Approach to Teaching* (San Francisco, CA: Jossey Bass, 2005).

25. Ibid., xii.

26. Ibid., 41–48.

27. Ibid., 1–37.

28. Ibid., 77–108.

29. Ibid., 151–169.

8

Don't Blame Teachers

Educational reformers, legislators, policymakers, and others enamored with the current slate of educational reform ideas never talk about things that get at the essence of teaching and learning. They think they do when they talk about standards, benchmarks, and standardized testing—when talk turns to whether or not teachers are actually teaching students what they are supposed to be teaching them, and whether or not they are doing it well enough. But not a word about academic clubs, or trafficking in truths, or perfection, or essential questions, or the meaningfulness of learning *ever* appears in the educational reform conversation. No such talk *ever* informs their ideas about the efforts and effectiveness of teachers, the purposes of education, or teacher evaluation. That's because you can't get to the ideas of Smith, Jackson, Gardner, and Egan (and others) when all you think about is how and why teachers should be blamed for the state of our schools and resented for the indifferent disregard, contempt, and malevolence you believe they aim directly toward students and toward us. When you start with blame and resentment, you end up railing about teacher tenure, teacher unions, self-interested teachers, standardized tests,

Blame Teachers, pages 131–137
131

charter schools, and ways to shape-up everybody and everything in accord with a small set of social ideas. Blame and resentment are blinders and noise deflectors usually worn by people too far outside the classroom to see and appreciate deeper and more intimate aspects of teaching and learning.

We will rue the day when blame and resentment began to orient the conversation about schools, teaching, and learning. We should already regret it. We should worry that so many of our best teachers have left the profession, or are thinking of leaving it, because of these reforms. Teaching isn't as gratifying as it used to be. Standards, pressure to raise test scores, being "managed" by instructional leaders, determining teaching effectiveness by value-added measures—none of these things encourage our best teachers to stay in the classroom. And we should worry that these same things will discourage our "best and brightest" young people from entering the profession—the people Duncan and Kopp want to attract to the profession. These quality people will find something else to do where they won't be "managed," mistreated, and mistrusted. We might also regret getting rid of tenure for teachers. We'll be much less proud of this educational reform when in the future we can't attract the good, solid people into teaching that we used to attract—those for whom community, stability, security, and quiet modesty are not hateful virtues or nasty words.

We will regret how these reforms cheapen teaching and learning. When the teacher who seizes on the mandated standards and regularly practices her students on objectives derived from them "wins," and the teacher who concentrates more on pulling her students into her learning club in a meaningful way "loses"—that is, when the one is valued, congratulated, and rewarded for high test scores and the other is slapped with a low teacher evaluation score—teaching and learning suffer. Everything gets corrupted. Under pressure from this battery of reforms, we no longer see teaching and learning as a complex whole—a puzzling, confusing, fascinating, dynamic, and fragile event. Instead, as I suggested earlier, learning becomes an addition problem, and teaching is merely a process of getting students to the largest sum of learning possible. Socrates and his students seeking after the truth of things together, or teachers wanting students to understand themselves in terms of the subject matters they teach—such ideals are all but lost to us. Jackson's ideal of "perfection" makes no sense in the scheme of these reforms.

Perhaps we will regret these reforms as we continue to see entering college students quite practiced in basic skills, but absolutely unable to see, feel, or emotionally grasp the important ideas in their subject fields. Or, maybe we won't. In his 1987 book *The Closing of the American Mind*, Allan Bloom lamented that *eros*—that gnawing, mad desire to learn and to know—was lame even in the best of our college students.[1] He had all but given up on the rest of them. But, now, we don't even think about the *eros* of our students—and most of us have long since lost that mad, searing, and unquenchable desire to know. Besides, we have life options, power, and economic gods with which to frame our educational tasks. And teachers certainly don't have time to nurture this kind of desire in students. They are too busy making sure all their students meet the mandated standards in time for the test at the end of the year.

There are, however, some criticisms of teachers and some reform ideas that teachers should take seriously, whether they want to or not. It really is hard to justify a long, cumbersome process to fire teachers who have made egregious professional errors, some of these processes involving 20 or more steps (if the stories are true). And it's just as hard to justify offering teachers tenure after just a year or two of teaching. Teachers might find an audience more willing to accept tenure if teachers were observed and evaluated longer before a tenure offer was made—even four or five years, as in many states. Teachers also need to break the code of silence to which they often assent—the code that says "I won't tell you how to teach, and I won't say anything about what is going on in your classroom, if you don't say anything about what is going on in mine." Teachers need to find ways to talk to and help one another, and they need to police their own ranks. And it is also no doubt healthy for teachers to rethink assessment practices in light of talk about standards and benchmarks. I've detailed my worries about standards and all that come with them, but one thing that comes with standards talk is a real question about what is more important—what students really know and can do, or what amount of points students have amassed in the teacher's gradebook.

Teacher educators have some rethinking to do, as well. Teacher educators are in a tough place—besieged by their own slew of standards and accountability measures from state and national accrediting agencies and charged with preparing teachers to work in public schools where the limited vision of teaching we have been describing reigns supreme. There is a truth of teaching and learning reflected in this limited vision of teaching—that learning requires clarity about what is to be learned and what quality is acceptable—and many teacher educators embrace this truth. It can shape their own teaching and the arguments about teaching they make to their students. Many teacher educators buy into many or all of the proposed and implemented reforms. Not so for most foundations of education professors. These teacher educators are typically among the ones leading the argument against these reforms—usually the leftist critique I suggested in the Introduction that mostly worries about capitalistic motives of reformers and the assault on social justice. Teacher educators can also focus on teacher preparation issues that have little or nothing to do with these reforms—things like learning styles, multiple intelligences, "critical thinking," cooperative learning, or how to teach students from diverse backgrounds. Special methods instructors focus much of their attention on teaching techniques that work best with particular aspects of their subject matter.

All this is well and good, but far too many students leave their teacher education programs without doing any of the thinking I argued for in the last chapter. The "Why do we need to learn this?" question I posed at the beginning of Chapter 7 is certainly not the only question that could lead teacher educators, teacher education students, and practicing teachers to do a whole lot of serious thinking about teaching and learning, but it is a good start. It is also the kind of question that, if thought about and answered well, would lead to improved student performance. Students who know why they should care about a subject, or a piece of a subject, will have a reason to learn it. As I suggested at the end of the last chapter, the good and compelling answers teachers start to give to these questions will be a true mark of teacher effectiveness, and the time and energy teachers devote to finding these answers and embedding them in their teaching will be a real mark of their professional effort.

Teachers need time, encouragement, and support to do the kind of thinking suggested by Frank Smith, Kieran Egan and the others we discussed. It isn't always easy for a teacher to find for herself what is emotionally engaging or meaningful in a given subject matter, much less how to present that to a group of students not nearly as much "in the club" as she is. Human hopes, fears, and passions, or the "essential question," or even which horizontal, vertical, or elliptical track the teacher should take her students on—these aren't easy to think about, either. But we don't offer teachers a structured and supportive environment in which to do this thinking and make corresponding changes to their teaching. We have other things in mind for them.

Final Thoughts

Teachers aren't perfect. There are teachers who are not effective enough and teachers who don't put forth enough effort. There are teachers who lose their way in subject matter and lose sight of what they really need to accomplish with students. There are teachers who harm students and need to be removed from the classroom, and there are teachers who need oversight or mentoring. But just because we admit these things does not mean we should automatically embrace the reforms being proposed and implemented. This set of reforms indicts *all* teachers—it changes things for *every* teacher; it's blame and resentment spread everywhere.

It isn't strange to think about "perfection" in regard to teachers, even though we know teachers can't be perfect, and we know we can't expect them to be. The ideal of perfection came up in our reflections about effectiveness, and it is suggested in phrases like "whatever it takes" and "failure is not an option." But in a very real sense, educational reformers have taken perfection off the table. We don't talk about it anymore because we have so many lesser ways of describing teachers and teaching. We're much more comfortable talking about "competent" teachers, and "measuring" their effectiveness, and comparing teachers based on data. We want teachers to learn new things and remedy their "deficiencies," and we want them to worry about improving their "growth score." Now, we have teachers worrying about the number a wandering administrator "objectively" assigns them on the brand new teacher evaluation rubric a school or district has decided to use (now handily available on the administrator's Ipad for his ten-minute visit to the teacher's classroom). We want them to worry about satisfying the demands their "manager" might make of them. None of this requires the ideal of perfection. That ideal has dropped away, a victim of our confidence in numbers to describe teachers and teaching; and a victim, too, of our being so sure that teachers are lazy and disinterested. We don't believe teachers will improve their teaching because they aspire to perfection—we believe they will only work to improve their teaching to keep from getting fired.

But we have this *all* wrong. This just isn't how teachers think about and judge themselves. A truly gifted teacher doesn't want to be called "competent," and getting high ratings on "indicators" means next to nothing. Teachers don't aspire to meet some arbitrary standard set for them that doesn't begin to articulate what they want for students. The judgments teachers make about their own teaching have little or nothing to do with their most recent value-added score—and it has nothing to do with whether that score was higher or lower than the scores of their colleagues.

For anyone still moved by the lofty ideals of teaching, these are sick and sad ways of describing the effectiveness of a teacher. Most teachers have a higher standard. Most teachers know that perfection is *exactly* the standard by which they should be judged. They know this because that's the standard by which they judge themselves. Being good enough for teachers is like being good enough as a parent. It simply won't do. Only perfection will do—a daunting challenge, but children and students deserve it. And what does "being perfect" mean for teachers? Among other things, it means always providing exactly what students want and need when they want and need it. It means knowing exactly what to say and when to say it, and it means setting up an environment where students can thrive. It means never doing anything, even accidentally, that can hurt or damage students. It means having patience in really taxing situations. It means having thorough subject matter knowledge and knowing what pieces of the subject matter fit-in where. It means knowing exactly how to move learning along. It means taking time and energy to respond to student work. And mostly, it means giving yourself over to someone else. It's something so simple as thinking to say some little unrehearsed thing—an aside, maybe, or a personal reflection—so that students can begin to see something important in what they are studying; and it's something so big as knowing just when, and just how, to step into a very serious problem a student might be having.

There's just one problem: none of us does this perfectly. None of us does *any* of this perfectly—not as parents and not as teachers. Teachers live with failure every day, just like parents do—their own personal failure to do for students what those students most need them to do. They live with failure from moment to moment during the course of a lesson—realizing too late, for instance, that they failed to pick-up on a student comment or that they accidently hurt the feelings of a student with something they said. No lesson ever comes off perfectly, and even when lessons go well, teachers have no time to congratulate themselves. There's always the next moment to manage—more subject matter to prepare or present, a new range of decisions to make about what students need and can accept—and a new possibility the teacher won't live up to her own expectations. Failure is always just around the corner. And teachers make mistakes—sometimes big ones. Usually no one feels worse about a given mistake than the teacher who makes it. No one feels her imperfection more than a teacher at the end of a school day, or a school year, who thinks back on all the things she should have done differently.

But apparently we no longer believe teachers think this way. Or we don't think regular public school teachers think this way—just the young Teach for America cadets. Apparently we think that what I just wrote is a kind of self-congratulatory fiction public school teachers tell themselves, that nothing of the sort ever runs through their minds—they being too interested in making things easy for themselves. We have, at any rate, lined up a set of reforms and made a commitment to remake teaching based on an opposite sentiment or understanding—reforms based on blame and resentment, not respect and appreciation. That's bad enough, but the tragedy is that these reforms will quite likely make things worse for students (and teachers), not better.

Blame and resentment send us down the wrong paths in our thinking about the public schools, teachers, and teaching. There are better paths to take, and we need to take them now.

Note

1. Allan Bloom, *The Closing of the American Mind: How Higher Education has Failed Democracy and Impoverished the Souls of Today's Students* (New York, NY: Simon and Schuster, 1987), 132.

APPENDIX

Working Toward "Wow"

A Vision for a New Teaching Profession

Remarks of Arne Duncan,
National Board of Professional Teaching Standards

July 29, 2011

Thanks for having me. It's a real honor to be addressing an organization that has done so much to strengthen America's most important profession.

I don't look at newspaper cartoons much, but someone showed me one the other day that got me thinking. It showed a sports fantasy camp with a bunch of athletes standing around waiting to get an autograph from a short, balding guy. One player points to him and says, "I wish I had that kind of money and respect..." Another athlete points to the man and says, "Wow! (pause) A teacher!"

Now this was just a Sunday cartoon—and I know that you're not all short and balding—but the message behind the humor says a lot about America today:

We worship our athletes, our entertainers, our movie stars—but it is great teachers who really should trigger a 'wow.'

Blame Teachers, pages 139–147
Copyright © 2015 by Information Age Publishing
All rights of reproduction in any form reserved.

Standing in front of you today, I am wowed. There are so many teachers in this room who are igniting curiosity, inspiring passions and opening doors for students all across America. You stand at the summit of one of the hardest, most challenging professions. And your record speaks loudly. Although National Board Certified teachers are only 3% of the teaching force, you account for fully 20% of the 2011 Teachers of the Year. The educators in this room have changed thousands of lives for the better and I couldn't be prouder to address you.

(¶ 5) Teaching must be one of our nation's most honorable professions. Teachers help mold the future every day, having an impact that far outlasts any lesson plan or career. When I meet young people who want to make a difference, change a life, and leave behind a living, breathing legacy, I urge them to teach. Too often, though, bright, committed young Americans—the very people our students need in the classroom—do not answer the call to teach. Instead, they choose fields like law, medicine, and engineering—that command higher pay and often more respect.

Today, I want to talk about how we can change this trend, transform the teaching profession, and ensure that the next generation of teachers is the very best we can offer our children. I want to talk about how that Sunday morning cartoon can become a reality. I want to ask how outstanding educators like you can be the norm.

Back home in Chicago, I worked closely with our union and with a non-profit organization called the Chicago Public Education Fund to dramatically increase the number of National Board Certified teachers. It was a wonderful public private partnership. When I started as CEO in 2001, there were about 30,000 teachers in the district—but only 11 were NBCT's. When I left in 2009, there were nearly 1,200 NBCT's. I didn't encourage only the best teachers to apply. I encouraged everyone to apply because I knew that everyone benefits from professional development and feedback, regardless of whether or not you achieve certification.

National Board Certification forces teachers to understand their strengths and weaknesses and to learn how to get better. It helps teachers get to the truth behind the craft and understand what it really takes to inspire children to learn. And it completely demonstrates to our students the importance of being lifelong learners—all of you are walking the walk, and leading by example.

I'm also excited to see that the National Board for Professional Teaching Standards is helping develop policy around teacher evaluation. The "Student Learning, Student Achievement" report you released this March was a big step in the right direction. Teaching is demanding, difficult work.

You are called upon to make scores of decisions every day. Developing an evaluation system that recognizes the complexity of teaching and the full range of challenges will not be easy—which is why most current evaluation systems are so flawed. Too many states and districts have taken the easy way out—and simply shirked their responsibility.

(¶ 10) But, we can no longer pretend that all teachers or all principals are from Lake Wobegon where everyone is above average. It is time to recognize and reward our best teachers, support those in the middle, and also acknowledge that teaching may not be the best career choice for a small minority of teachers who continue to struggle despite support and mentorship. Teaching is not a job for everyone.

I'm especially pleased to learn that a new report you are about to issue recommends that teacher evaluation include measures of student learning and I thank you for taking that important step. In the twenty-first century, we shouldn't be guessing whether or not a teacher is impacting student learning—we should know—and while we know that the current generation of tests are far from perfect, a new generation is in development that will be better. You know this profession. You know what fair evaluation could look like. You know that it shouldn't be based only on bubble tests. You know that it should include multiple measures—like principal observation, peer review, parent and student feedback, student work, teacher attendance and other factors.

Let me be crystal clear. Neither the President nor I believe test scores should be the sole component of evaluation. We always have and always will support multiple measures. Test score growth and gain should be part of the equation in classrooms and subjects where they are available, but they should never be the only part.

Now I also know some people believe that factors outside the classroom—like poverty and family breakdown—can minimize or negate the positive impact that teachers have on students. They say that if a child comes from a broken home, it is unfair to expect that student to compete with classmates from more supportive environments. They also say it is unfair to hold teachers, principals, schools, or districts accountable for the achievement levels of those low-income students. I respect their opinion and appreciate their voice.

We know that poverty matters, but a teacher matters too. I have seen the extraordinary impact of great educators and great schools on the lives of children. I've worked all my life with children from poverty-stricken, violence-plagued communities. And I know that poverty is not destiny. We have all seen lives change because of opportunity, support, and guidance.

Yes, children all start at different places and bring different strengths, challenges and needs—and we can't hold teachers accountable for the skills of students when they walk in the door in September. But it is our collective responsibility to do whatever it takes to graduate that child from high school prepared for college or a career. Closing achievement gaps, by closing opportunity gaps, is the civil rights challenge of our generation.

(¶ 15) I don't pretend that poverty is not a factor. It's just not an excuse for students failing to make progress over the course of the school year. By measuring student growth instead of proficiency and by training our principals and evaluators to recognize these out-of-school factors and take them into account, we can have a richer, more meaningful and fairer system of accountability. So today I welcome the efforts of the National Board for Professional Teaching Standards. I look forward to reading your new report and taking the next step together.

The urgency to get better has never been greater. The world is rapidly moving forward while America is standing still. Moreover, the field of teaching is poised for change. Roughly half of America's 3.2 million active teachers could retire by the end of this decade. As baby boomers move towards retirement, we will have real challenges and real opportunity. We have an amazing chance to modernize the teaching profession and expand the talent pool.

But it will require dramatic changes in the way we recruit, train, support, evaluate and compensate teachers. And there are important lessons from abroad. In nearly every leading country, a large majority of teachers come from the top third of college graduates. That must be our goal as well. The countries that are beating us in the classroom today will beat us in the workplace tomorrow—so this is a matter of economic security and national security. To win the future, we must mirror these high-performing countries and recruit more teachers from the top third.

Many bright and committed young people are attracted to teaching, but surveys show they are reluctant to enter the field for the long-haul. They see it as low-paying and low-prestige. They want excellence to be rewarded and meaningful feedback provided. They want a job that requires top-flight credentials and a challenging work schedule. They want autonomy, the time and space to be creative, and they are willing to be held accountable. But they don't look at teaching the way they look at law, medicine or engineering. It requires too many sacrifices that other professions don't have to make.

The national call to professionalize teaching is almost as old as the field itself. In 1958, then Senator John F. Kennedy wrote a piece in the NEA Journal calling for revitalizing the field of teaching. In 1984, legendary leader Albert Shanker said that attracting and retaining good teachers is "the major struggle in education." In 1986, the Carnegie Report called for a new teaching profession. Ten years later, the National Commission on Teaching and America's Future issued a report called "What Matters Most"—which talked about professionalizing the field.

(¶ 20) Matt Miller—a journalist and policy expert wrote a book a few years ago called the "Two Percent Solution" arguing for a new paradigm in teaching. He also called for dramatically higher teacher salaries as a way to attract top students. Last year, McKinsey did a study comparing the U.S. to other countries and recommending—among other things—that we change the economics of the profession, pointing out that entry-level salary in the high 30's and an average ceiling in the high 60's will never attract and retain the top talent.

We must think radically differently. We should also be asking how the teaching profession might change if salaries started at $60,000 and rose to $150,000. We must ask and answer hard questions on topics that have been off limits in the past like staffing practices and school organization, benefits packages and job security—because the answers may give us more realistic ways to afford these new professional conditions. If teachers are to be treated and compensated as the true professionals they are, the profession will need to shift away from an industrial-era blue-collar model of compensation to rewarding effectiveness and performance. Money is never the reason why people enter teaching, but it is the reason why some people do not enter teaching, or leave as they start to think about beginning a family and buying a home. Today, too often the heart-breaking reality is that a good teacher with a decade of classroom experience is hard-pressed to raise a family on a teacher's salary. That must change.

There is a new movie called *American Teacher* coming out produced by the writer Dave Eggers and a teacher, Ninive Caligari, profiling several outstanding teachers.

One of them drives a forklift at night to support his family—and eventually the pressure of two jobs costs him his marriage. Another teacher in the movie—an African-American male elementary school teacher—finally quits and goes into real estate where he earns twice as much, working half as hard. When we are losing talented, passionate educators like this, the profession is in crisis. Fully, half of the people who go into teaching leave within five years. Lack of support, lack of quality mentoring and meaningful professional development, inadequate respect and compensation—we know the reasons. That is unsustainable in any field, let alone something as important as teaching. And in high-poverty schools where the most committed, accomplished teachers are needed, the salaries are often lower. Data collected by our team in the Office for Civil Rights indicates that in high-poverty schools, turnover is higher and experience levels are lower. There are great teachers in these schools—just not enough of them; not enough of a critical mass.

So the incentives today are all wrong—not just the money but the prestige and the career opportunities. We need to agree that in teaching, as in every skilled profession—medicine, business, the arts—quality matters. There's a huge gulf of greatness and grit separating our best teachers from our worst. Today, too many schools and districts evaluate, recognize, and compensate teachers without respect to their impact on student learning. This is an assembly-line model of pay, based on seniority and educational credentials.

This is not how professionals are compensated in this age of innovation. Top undergraduates want to know that their talent and hard work will be rewarded.

They want to know that their commitment is meaningful and recognized. If it isn't, great potential teachers will find that their skills, passion, and creativity have greater value elsewhere.

(¶ 25) Teachers absolutely need and deserve the autonomy that other highly accomplished professionals enjoy. The hospital administrator doesn't hover over a world-class surgeon. The managing partner of a law firm doesn't hover over the firm's top litigator. Instead, they get them the tools, resources, and support they need to be successful today and to continue to learn and grow. As we get great talent in the classroom, we must trust them to make decisions like every other profession . . . and then hold them accountable.

We also need to raise the bar for entry in the field. Top undergraduates will flock to a profession that demands high standards and credentials. Yet, too many of our nation's 1,400 schools of education lack the rigor to attract talented students.

And to see how this change might happen, we can look to the field of medicine for a fascinating example—from 100 years ago. In 1910, medicine was in disarray. Medical schools didn't even require a high school diploma. Medical preparation consisted of two years of guest lecturers with virtually no hospital experience.

The schools varied wildly in quality. Almost any applicant who could pay the tuition was accepted. Medical schools were cash cows for universities—and doesn't that sound familiar. Along came an educator named Abraham Flexner who visited all 155 medical schools and published his findings. He called for higher standards for people charged with saving lives—and helped launch a new era in the field of medicine. He told the truth and the world changed.

In the field of education, we also need to tell the truth. We all need to say out loud what everyone knows: the field of education must change, grow, improve, and rise to a higher standard of professionalism. You are not just saving lives, like doctors, you are also helping create lives of hope and opportunity.

(¶ 30) This conference is called "Reboot! Teaching Transformed." I know that you're primarily referring to the use of technology in the classroom—and I know you heard from one of my top advisors Karen Cator. Technology—in partnership with great teaching—can really help teachers get better and boost student outcomes. But if we're truly going to transform American education, we must go far beyond the smart use of technology. We must remake the teaching profession itself. We must think big. Our children, our parents, our teachers, and our country deserve better.

In too many ways the current model no longer works: a broken pipeline, a nine-month school year based on the agrarian economy, a factory approach to staffing, compensation and benefits, a school design from the last century, and a management structure that is simply not up to the challenge. Too many principals and administrators are falling down on the job when it comes to mentoring, evaluating and supporting teachers. Too many are simply overwhelmed with bureaucratic burdens and political pressures to be the real instructional leaders we need them to be. And we are absolutely part of the problem too. Education officials at the state and federal level need to narrow their role, and get out of the way as much as possible, while holding ourselves and each other accountable for educational equity and quality. Instead of being a compliance-driven bureaucracy, we should be an engine of innovation, fostering new approaches and ideas. We must be more flexible—focused more on goals than on means. We must look in the mirror every day, and ask ourselves, are we perpetuating the problem, or creating the solutions?

So I'm here today to challenge us all to work together towards one profound goal: to make teaching one of our nation's most venerated professions. In Singapore and South Korea teachers are known as "nation-builders." Think what that would mean to all of us, if America's teachers were recognized as "nation-builders." Let's get out of the box we've been stuck in for decades—and picture a day when highly accomplished teach-

ers are considered masters in their fields and compensated accordingly—
and where they don't need to become administrators or leave teaching in
order to support their families. We should keep our best teachers in the
classroom—and they should be earning a lot more money—as much as
$150,000 per year. Let's face it: a phenomenal teacher educating under-
served kids in science, technology, math, engineering, or the arts should be
very well compensated—just as they are in other professions. A kindergarten teacher who can turn every child into a reader is priceless.

Picture a day when all teachers have access to strong mentors, good
incentive programs, meaningful professional development, and real career
ladders. Picture a day when teachers are evaluated like other professionals,
using multiple sources of evidence about their success on the job. Picture
a day when all teachers—not just three percent—aspire to the high and
rigorous standards achieved by all of you here today. Picture a day when an
entry-level teacher's salary is radically higher—especially in a low-income
and low-performing school—and when a top undergraduate walks off the
stage and says to his mother, "Mom—I'm going to be a highly respected,
well-paid professional. I'm going to be a teacher."

Earlier this month, I met with thirteen amazing former state teachers
of the year to talk about elevating the teaching profession. Like you—these
teachers are at the top of their field. We didn't agree on everything—but
we all recognized the urgent need for change in the profession. They are
not afraid of it. In fact, they are begging for it and want to work together
to make it happen. They want us all to come together and deal openly
and honestly with the challenges and choices needed to bring about real
transformation. They are hungry for a vigorous national conversation—led
by teachers—about the profession that our children need and that good
teachers want. They expect some noisy debates—and they know it won't
happen overnight. It won't happen everywhere at once. It will require everyone to go outside their comfort zones.

(¶ 35) And it will cost money—and—given the current political climate
with the nation wrestling with debt and deficits—I am sure some people
will immediately say that we can't afford it without even looking at how to
redirect the money we are already spending—and miss-spending. To them
I say that there is more than one way to mortgage your future. We can't
mortgage our future by under-investing in education.

Still others will hear the message about tradeoffs in terms of job security or benefits, and try to suppress the kind of open dialogue we need
about the teaching profession. I respectfully urge everyone to take a deep
breath, hold their fire, and see this as an opportunity to transform the en-

tire profession—not as a threat or as an investment we don't need. We respectfully need it. This isn't just coming from me—or some narrow segment of the reform community. This is coming from thousands of great teachers all across America who desperately want our respect, our support, and our trust. This professional transformation won't happen unless teachers own this and drive this. Change can only come from the men and women who do the hard work every day in our classrooms.

This group, Nationally Board Certified Teachers, has always stood for excellence and professionalism. You are uniquely prepared to take on this mission and transform your field. So, I urge you to lead this effort. Your colleagues in the classroom trust you. They will take your lead and they will follow you. Appeal to their highest ideals. Bring their voice into the conversation, and help them see that by taking full responsibility for their profession, they can remake it in their own eyes—and in the eyes of our nation.

And then we can all look forward to the day when people across society who meet a teacher come away with just one word on their lips: "Wow."

Thank you.

Bibliography

Bloom, A. (1987). *The closing of the American mind: How higher education has failed democracy and impoverished the souls of today's students*. New York, NY: Simon and Schuster.

Brookover, W., Beamer, L., Efthim, H., Hathaway, D., Lezotte, L., Miller, S., Passalacqua J., & Tornatzky, L. (1982). *Creating effective schools*. Holmes Beach, FL: Learning.

Bush, G. (2001). *Address to a joint session of congress and the American people*. Accessed January 14, 2015. http://georgewbush-whitehouse.archives.gov/news/releases/2001/09/20010920-8.html

Center for Research on Education Outcomes. (2013). *National charter school study 2013*. Accessed January 15, 2015. http://credo.stanford.edu/documents/NCSS%202013%20Final%20Draft.pdf.

Christie, C. (2011). *2011: The year of education reform*. Accessed October 25, 2014. http://www.brookings.edu/events/2011/04/07-education-christie.

Coleman, J. S., Campbell, E. Q., Hobson, C. J., McPartland, J., Mood, A. M., Weinfeld, R. D., & York, R. L. (1966). *Equality of educational opportunity*. Washington, DC: U.S. Department of Health, Education and Welfare, FS 5.238.38001.

College Board. (2014). *2012 College-bound seniors total group profile report*. Accessed October 25, 2014. http://media.collegeboard.com/digitalServices/pdf/research/TotalGroup-2012.pdf.

Collins, J. (2001). *Good to great: Why some companies make the leap . . . and others don't*. New York, NY: HarperBusiness.

Cusick, P. (2007). Why do kids hate school? Why do we care?" In S. P. Jones, C. J. Pearman, & E. C. Sheffield (Eds.), *Why kids hate school* (pp. 4–5). Dubuque, IA: Kendall/Hunt.

Blame Teachers, pages 149–151
Copyright © 2015 by Information Age Publishing
All rights of reproduction in any form reserved.

District of Columbia Public Schools. (2014). *An overview of IMPACT.* Accessed October 25, 2014. http://dcps.dc.gov/DCPS/In+the+Classroom/Ensuring +Teacher+Success/IMPACT+(Performance+Assessment)/An+Overview +of+IMPACT.

Duncan, A. (2011). *Working toward "wow": A vision for a new teaching profession.* Accessed October 25, 2014. http://www.ed.gov/news/speeches/working-toward-wow-vision-new-teaching-profession.

Educational Testing Service. (2015). *GRE guide to the use of scores.* Accessed October 25, 2014. www.ets.org/gre/institutions/scores/interpret/.

Effective Schools. (2012). *Learning for all.* Accessed October 25, 2014. http://www.effectiveschools.com/.

Egan, K. (2005). *An imaginative approach to teaching.* San Francisco, CA: Jossey Bass.

Gardner, H. (2000). *The disciplined mind: Beyond facts and standardized tests, the K–12 education that every child deserves.* New York, NY: Penguin Books.

Gardner, H. (2011). *Truth, beauty, and goodness reframed: Educating for the virtues in the twenty-first century.* New York, NY: Basic Books.

Gray, D., & Weinberg, J. (2009). *The blame game.* Accessed October 25, 2014. http://www.ayeconference.com/the-blame-game/.

Greene, J. P. (2011). *Why America needs school choice.* New York, NY: Encounter Books.

Hansen, D. (1995). *The call to teach.* New York, NY: Teachers College Press.

Horn, J. (2012). A Former KIPP Teacher Shares Her Story. *Schools Matter.* Accessed October 25, 2014. http://www.schoolsmatter.info/2012/09/a-former-kipp-teacher-shares-her-story.html.

Institute of Education Sciences. (2014). What Works Clearinghouse. Accessed October 25, 2014. http://ies.ed.gov/ncee/wwc/.

Internet Encyclopedia of Philosophy. (2014). Francis Bacon, 1561–1626). Accessed October 25, 2014. http://www.iep.utm.edu/bacon/.

Jackson, P. (2012). *What is education?* Chicago, IL: University of Chicago Press.

Jackson, P. W., Boostrom, R. E., & Hansen, D. T. (1998). *The moral life of schools.* San Francisco, CA: Jossey-Bass.

Jencks, C., Smith, M., Acland, H., Bane, M. J., Cohen, D., Gintis, H., Heyns, B., & Michelson, S. (1972). *Inequality: A reassessment of the effect of family and schooling in America.* New York, NY: Basic Books.

Knowledge is Power Program. (2014a). *Excellent teaching.* Accessed October 25, 2014. http://www.kipp.org/our-approach/excellent-teaching.

Knowledge is Power Program. (2014b). *How we do it.* Accessed October 25, 2014. http://kipp.org/our-approach.

Knowledge is Power Program. (2014c). *How we do it—Five pillars.* Accessed October 25, 2014. http://www.kipp.org/our-approach/five-pillars.

Knowledge is Power Program. (2014d). *KIPP framework for excellent teaching.* Accessed October 25, 2014. http://www.kipp.org/files/dmfile/07022012KFET.pdf.

Knowledge is Power Program. (2014e). *Where will you take us?* Accessed October 25, 2014. http://www.kipp.org/careers/applicant-faqs.

Kopp, W. (2011). *A chance to make history: What works and what doesn't in providing an excellent education for all.* New York, NY: Public Affairs.

McGraw-Hill Dictionary of Idioms and Phrasal Verbs. (2002). New York, NY: The McGraw-Hill Companies, Inc.

Missouri Department of Elementary and Secondary Education. (2013). *Teacher evaluation.* Accessed October 25, 2014. http://dese.mo.gov/sites/default/files/01-TeacherEvaluationProtocol.pdf.

National Commission on Excellence in Education. (1983). *A nation at risk.* Ann Arbor: University of Michigan Library.

Owen, D. (2007). Why do kids hate school? A question of context. In S. P. Jones, C. J. Pearman, & E. C. Sheffield (Eds.), *Why kids hate school* (pp. 29–30). Dubuque, IA: Kendall/Hunt.

Pope, D. (2003). *Doing school: How we are creating a generation of stressed-out, materialistic, and miseducated students.* New Haven, CT: Yale University Press.

Postman, N. (1995). *The end of education: Redefining the value of school.* New York, NY: Alfred A. Knopf.

Ravitch, D. (2011). *The death and life of the great American school system: How testing and choice are undermining education.* New York, NY: Basic Books.

Shaw, G. B. (1962). Maxims for revolutionists. *Bernard Shaw: Complete plays with prefaces.* New York, NY: Dodd, Mead & Company.

Smith, F. (1998). *The book of learning and forgetting.* New York, NY: Teachers College Press.

Strawson, P. F. (1962). Freedom and resentment. *Proceedings of the British Academy 48,* 1–25. Accessed October 25, 2014. http://people.brandeis.edu/~teuber/P._F._Strawson_Freedom_&_Resentment.pdf.

Teach for America. (2014). *Compensation and benefits.* Accessed October 25, 2014. http://www.teachforamerica.org/why-teach-for-america/compensation-and-benefits.

Tennessee Department of Education. (2014). *TEAMTN.* Accessed October 25, 2014. http://team-tn.org/.

Tyack, D. (1974). *The one best system: A history of American urban education.* Boston, MA: Harvard University Press.

U.S. Department of Education. (2014). *Race to the top.* Accessed October 25, 2014. http://www2.ed.gov/programs/racetothetop/index.html.

Whitmire, R. (2011). *Education is the new abortion: The battle over school reform has turned dangerously vitriolic.* NYDailyNews.com. Accessed October 25, 2014. http://www.nydailynews.com/opinion/education-new-abortion-battle-school-reform-turned-dangerously-vitriolic-article-1.132343.

Acknowledgments

Many experiences, and many people, have shaped my desire to write this book, especially my experiences as a student, a teacher and a colleague of many wonderful teachers. First of all, I remember teachers who meant so much to me: Jack Fredericksen, my band and jazz band director at Lincoln High School in Denver, Colorado; Vincent LaGuardia, Jr., my orchestra conductor from junior high school through college; and Edward Twining and Douglas Wilson from the English department at the University of Denver. I was privileged to work with Jim Starkey (and his wife, Kathy) during my student teaching experience at Green Mountain High School, and I was privileged, as well, to work with dedicated colleagues in the English department at Lakewood High School, just west of Denver—especially Ann Klaiman, Janet Zamboni, Jerilynn Sullivan, and Luanne Pendorf. Teachers in my graduate programs at the University of Colorado and the University of Chicago have also inspired this book—people like Russell Meyers (from Colorado) and Philip Jackson, Allan Bloom and Joseph Cropsey (from Chicago). And graduate school brought me colleagues I'm now privileged to call friends, especially Klaus Amburn, Gerald Pillsbury, Rene Arcilla, David Hansen, and Robert Boostrom.

Many of the ideas in this book were worked out in front of my students at Missouri State University. Special thanks go to Stephanie (Coulter) Hotz and Marci Johnson, ex-students and now dear friends, who encouraged me during the course of writing this book. Thanks also go out to Eric Sheffield, my dear friend and colleague at MSU. Parts of this argument have been

Blame Teachers, pages 153–154
Copyright © 2015 by Information Age Publishing
All rights of reproduction in any form reserved.

presented at Critical Questions in Education conferences—CQiE being a national conference put together by the Academy for Educational Studies. Thanks, also, to all the people at Information Age Press, especially John Petrovic, the editor of the Philosophy of Education section of IAP.

The book is dedicated to my parents, now deceased, who always supported, in words and acts, my being a teacher. And it is dedicated to my wife, Jackie, who encourages and helps me in everything I do. These three people have had a hand in everything good I've ever done.

And one more thing. Philip Jackson told me something about writing that I've never forgotten. Everything you write, he said, is both a success and a failure. It is a success for what it says well, gracefully, and clearly, and for the insight and help it brings the reader. It is a failure for what it says clumsily or badly, and for what it should have said, but didn't. He told me I needed to get used to that, and his words have given me solace countless times as I have labored over this book. And so I tell you, the reader, that I accept responsibility for both the success and failure of this book.

Made in the USA
Lexington, KY
29 August 2016